WHERE DO I GO FROM HERE

**22 Conversations To Help You Survive
The Initial Phases of *Divorce***

Mariah Willis Strong

KEEN
VISION
PUBLISHING

Printed in the United States of America
Keen Vision Publishing, LLC
www.publishwithkvp.com
ISBN: 979-8-9912210-4-7

Thank you to my friends and family who walked with me through one of the most challenging seasons of my life. Thank you for your support and prayers.

CONVERSATIONS INSIDE
To be experienced in no particular order

Introduction	7
There Is Hope	11
It's Okay Not to be Okay	17
Have No Fear	23
Trust Yourself	29
Visits from Anger	35
Restored from Within	41
Trusting God's Nature	47
Getting Untangled	53
Pain and Heartache	59
You Need a Village	65
In Pursuit of Peace	71
You Win Some, You Learn Some	77
Remaining Present	83
Ready, Set, Heal!	89
Do You Hear That?	95
The Search for Better Days	101
Less Than Picture-Perfect	107
The Reality of Forgiveness	113

It's Only a Test 117

Decoding Grief 121

Guard Your Heart 127

Reframe Your Life 133

About the Author **139**

INTRODUCTION

Married and considering divorce?
Close this book. It isn't for you.

Hit a difficult patch in your marriage?
Close this book. It isn't for you.

Separated and seeking counseling?
Close this book. It isn't for you.

W*here Do I Go From Here?* was created for those who have felt the gut punch that knocks the wind out of you when you realize your marriage is over. It doesn't matter if you filed for divorce or were served. There is, or at least should be, an indescribable feeling when you recognize that what you thought would last forever has now come to an end.

For some, you were able to see the writing on the wall and have wondered for days or even years if this day would ever come. Others may have been caught completely off-guard by their spouse, who turned promises to cherish and love them into goals to crush and destroy. I was a mix between being in the know and being caught off guard; I didn't initially see the writing on the wall, but everything slowly revealed itself to me. Near the end, I could sense that the chamber that used to hold and protect my heart had become a crypt that held deceit and broken promises. I did what I thought any good Christian spouse should do: *Pray. Fast. Seek wise counsel. Pray. Fast. Believe. Confess. Pray.* However, it became apparent that I was the only one fighting for us.

my story

My son was six months old. I had just fed him and was preparing to bathe him and settle in for the night when I heard a knock at my door. It was dark, and I was home alone again, so I wasn't sure who it could be. I quickly glanced through my security system and assumed it was another solar panel salesman. I started to ignore him, but then he knocked again.

Considering this could be a delivery for myself or my husband, I answered the door with my chubby baby boy balanced on one hip. He verified my name, handed me a stack of papers, and said words I'd only heard in a movie: *"You've been served."* As he looked at my son and looked back at me, he put his head down and said, *"I'm sorry,"* as he walked away.

Disappointment, shame, defeat, sadness, anger, and disbelief — so many emotions travel through my mind. Before one could truly settle, another emerged. I share this small part of my story to say that I have been where you are and, unfortunately, am acquainted with what you are feeling. I understand how your feelings begin to contradict themselves, how your mind can't make sense of the conjoined emotions that course through your veins. I know what it is to take on the legal battle of a lifetime to defend what was created out of love with the best intentions, never once considering that you'd have to split things 50/50. But now, I also know what it feels like to be on the other side, and there is a process to get through it all.

find what you need

As you read this book, I pray that you will find encouragement, strength, and the ability to put one foot in front of the other while trusting God to hold you up when your knees buckle — because they will at some point. There will be a buckling in the greatest form of surrender you could ever imagine. Surrendering your past, present, and each breath of your future into the only hand that is big enough to hold us and our issues all at the same time.

These conversations I bring before you aren't meant to be linear or cyclical. They are more so intended to be as unpredictable as your feelings may be in the next 30, 60, or 90 days. Find the message that speaks to you that day, even if you stay in one conversation for a week. There will be Scriptures listed as **Sure Ground** to help you find your footing during this shaky time. Utilize Scriptures to remind yourself of the faithfulness and character of God during this season. Record the Scripture in your voice memos to play when words fail.

Prayers will be listed as **Draw Near**. The adversary of our souls would find such pleasure if we allow the temporary circumstance to persuade our hope in eternal glory. These are prayers that I have prayed myself, but feel free to make them personal to your situation. Journal prompts will allow space for you to **Stop, Reflect** *and Release.* Some topics will be more challenging than others. You may not be able to complete them the first time you read the prompt, but I challenge you to revisit it in time and contend for that place of peace.

Most importantly, **DO NOT GIVE UP.** There will be hard days. There will be dark days. Remember — this is only a page in your story, not the entire chapter or book. You will make it to the other side one day, moment, hour, minute, second at a time, My hope for you on this day and every day moving forward is that you are able to find the will to live, the faith to believe again, and the strength to trust that the same God who began a work in you will complete it until the day that Jesus Christ returns to take us home.

Despite how you may feel in this very moment, we serve a God who can make all things new. I look forward to seeing the new you!

THERE IS HOPE

Have you experienced having a CAT scan or MRI completed? If not, let me paint the picture for you. Before the exam can take place, you must remove any garments that have metal before donning a medical apron. You lay on a cold metal board, sometimes strapped down, in various positions that provide the best access to the injury. Once you are properly, not necessarily comfortably positioned, the metal table slides into a circular tube-like entrance that you aren't quite sure the table, much less a human body strapped to it, would fit without getting stuck.

For me, this is where things get interesting. I always inform the technician that I need to close my eyes before entering a slender tube for the procedure to be successful, which is typically the case. But on the few occasions that the technician forgot… Lord, have mercy! I almost tore up those folk's machine. Shutting my eyes after entering the tube, knowing how close I really was to the machine, brought to light that I have some level of claustrophobia as I could only imagine the tube closing tighter and tighter around me until I panicked. I know the exam serves a purpose in providing a diagnosis to ultimately help me heal. However, without assistance, I am not capable of completing the process.

That's also the best way I could describe the feeling of hopelessness. I've been stripped of protection and support. I know I've had an impactful life experience that I need to examine. Through that examination, I will be able to move toward healing. But hopelessness is like the tube of the MRI machine I wasn't prepared to enter, and although I can find healing on the other side, this tube of hopelessness feels as though it is closing in tighter and tighter. It may not be that way for everyone, but that was definitely my experience.

finding hope again

The enemy would love nothing more than for us to allow this temporary situation to have an eternal impact by choosing to walk away from the only one who can truly prepare us for the journey ahead. It finally clicked for me one day: For me to have lost hope would mean I did have something I initially hoped for. What, or who rather, was that hope? I had allowed my suffering to distract me from who God is, what He has done through Jesus Christ, and what that gives me access to. Even though this pain is real and fresh, the truth of the matter is – it won't last forever.

> Hope is being able to see that there is light despite all of the darkness.
>
> **DESMOND TUTU**

With that realization, renewing my mind daily became a top priority. I knew that if I was going to battle this way of thinking, I had to replace the negative and defeatist thoughts with thoughts of life and victory. I honestly didn't feel strong enough to sit and read Scripture. Instead, I played artists whose lyrics were verbatim or directly resembled Scripture. It was the first and last thing I would hear each day, to the point I would wake up singing certain lyrics in my head.

To continue this uphill battle, I knew prayer was essential. It was my way of forcing myself to verbally express all of the sweet blessings that had been mixed with this bitter experience. I listed them out one by one:

Thank you for my son.
Thank you for our health.
Thank you for Your provision.
Thank you for keeping us safe.
Thank you for waking us up today.
Thank you for a job that I enjoy.

Day by day, the list continued to grow and expand as I could literally feel life being breathed into me. This was my way of shining light into the darkness, refusing to be completely consumed. As the light continued to break through the darkness, I prayed that I would find joy in the promise of eternity as I did when I first accepted salvation through Jesus Christ. I asked for that faith and hope that I experienced on that day to be made fresh and new in this season of my life so I wouldn't forget where my focus should remain: on things that are true, noble, just, pure, lovely, and of good report (Philippians 4:8).

I have been to the depths of depression – *God found me there.* I have been at a place where not being here seemed like the best option – *God found me there.* I have sat in the same place for three days trying to find the strength to just shower – *God found me there.* God can do away with hopelessness. So, let's do away with seeking God once we are out of our situation, and instead, let's invite Him into the place where He has a track record of doing His best work – into the darkness.

sure ground

But those who trust in the LORD will find new strength. They will soar high on wings like eagles. They will run and not grow weary. They will walk and not faint.

ISAIAH 40:31

As for me, I look to the LORD for help. I wait confidently for God to save me, and my God will certainly hear me.

MICAH 7:7

For I know the plans I have for you," says the LORD. "They are plans for good and not for disaster, to give you a future and a hope.

JEREMIAH 29:11

I pray that God, the source of hope, will fill you completely with joy and peace because you trust in him. Then you will overflow with confident hope through the power of the Holy Spirit.

ROMANS 15:13

And now, dear brothers and sisters, one final thing. Fix your thoughts on what is true, and honorable, and right, and pure, and lovely, and admirable. Think about things that are excellent and worthy of praise.

PHILIPPIANS 4:8

stop, reflect & release

Do you feel a sense of hopelessness or depression? If so, what does that look like for you?

How can you renew your mind when darkness tries to creep in?

Each day, write five things you are grateful for.

draw near

Heavenly Father, thank you for the hope of eternal life with You that we have through salvation in Jesus Christ. Help me not to lose sight of that hope in the midst of this difficult time. Remind me of the plan and hope You have for my life. Renew my strength each day so that I don't grow weary or faint. Help me count each blessing as I resist the enemy, not leaving any space for him to settle in.

In Jesus' Name, Amen.

GOD
DOES HIS BEST WORK
IN THE DARK

IT'S OKAY NOT TO BE OKAY

As a former Division II student-athlete, I generally handled stress, pressure, and responsibilities reasonably well. I was 17 when I left home to play on a scholarship, which was a lot of responsibility for anyone, especially for a fresh 17-year-old. Those who've known me say I have an "old soul" and have always been mature for my age. That level of responsibility only increased as I progressed through my collegiate years and began working in my profession at the age of 23. Filing my taxes, completing my W2 forms, and figuring out a budget were pressures I wasn't sure I was so excited to have, yet as time progressed, I conquered them, and they didn't conquer me. Of course, these would not be the only pressures I had to fight against.

Fast-forward to November 2022. As I was scrambling to fight for my marriage, I figured I could use the same skill set of hard work, determination, and persistence to handle the reality of my marriage ending, swiftly approaching court dates, and being the sole caretaker for my small child. Whew, was I wrong. In fact, if I had continued running as hard and fast as I initially attempted, I don't believe the outcome would have been positive.

My attention began to drift, and I unleashed my anger on those who were only trying to help me. Most days concluded with seemingly endless tears as I tried to make sense of the uncertainty of our lives hanging in limbo. As much as I tried to soldier on, I slowly came to the realization that I was not okay. After a well-intended phone call from family to motivate me to dry my tears and prepare myself to move forward, I responded: "You know, I've been through A LOT. And even though I am going to force myself through this process, I'm not okay, and that is okay." In this world of pixilated perfections, it takes honesty, humility, and vulnerability to realize: a) there is a problem or issue, and b) I need help.

trauma is real

Trauma can be divided into two categories: Big "T" trauma that psychologists believe are events almost everyone would agree are traumatic. Little "t" trauma are events psychologists consider to be traumatic based on an individual's response, but the majority of people would not find them to be traumatic. Surprisingly to me, divorce is listed under little "t" trauma. I believe it is vital that we bring normalcy to the pain, grief, and emotional trauma that may be present before, during, in the midst of, and after a divorce. No matter how the marriage ended, at conception, it most likely was not the intention or hope of either party to get to this place of division. It is only through this recognition that we can begin our healing process. For me, the emotional trauma of my marriage ending was very real, so I had to become R.E.A.L. as well.

Recognize what I am feeling and identify my triggers.
Express the various emotions I was experiencing and put names to those feelings.
Allow my resources and family to help me so I can begin to heal.
Live life one moment, one day at a time, because considering anything further was too overwhelming.

I knew I had to deal with what was in front of me. In this process, I quickly realized that no matter how supportive my family continued to be, they had not walked the journey that I was facing. My family remained so supportive by showing up every time I called and empathizing with me, but something was still missing. I enlisted the help of a therapist, who I still meet with periodically, to help me reframe my thinking and put the course and recent events of my life into perspective. Therapists can be expensive; however, most employers now offer assistance programs that provide free or discounted counseling services.

Alongside my therapist, I had scheduled devotional time with a dear family friend and seasoned believer who held me accountable for remaining in the word of God and strengthened me with some encouragement of how various women and God navigated impactful situations. She also encouraged me to work hard towards forgiveness so that anger did not turn into bitterness. My OB-GYN and primary physician were as essential as the first two supports. I am so grateful that they properly assessed me and provided natural and pharmaceutical options that could benefit me during this major life transition. Medicinal supports have their place in recovery and don't have to be permanent resources. I found what worked best for me during this time.

As you progress through your own divorce process, you should revisit this chapter as a reminder that what you're facing is a difficult battle, but it isn't an impossible one. I encourage you to seek the help and resources to breathe life into you during this season. Know that this season will not last forever and that, in time, you will begin to see yourself healing and becoming whole again.

While working to accept your reality, remind yourself it is okay not to be okay. There may be things clouding your vision, but I hope you begin to see past the pain, trauma, and disappointment for yourself day by day. With God, you will get there in due time!

sure ground

God is our refuge and strength, always ready to help in times of trouble. So, we will not fear when earthquakes come and the mountains crumble into the sea. Let the oceans roar and foam. Let the mountains tremble as the waters surge!
PSALMS 46:1-3

But now, O Jacob, listen to the LORD who created you. O Israel, the one who formed you says, "Do not be afraid, for I have ransomed you. I have called you by name; you are mine. When you go through deep waters, I will be with you.

When you go through rivers of difficulty, you will not drown. When you walk through the fire of oppression, you will not be burned up; the flames will not consume you."

ISAIAH 43: 1-2

That is why we never give up. Though our bodies are dying, our spirits are being renewed every day. For our present troubles are small and won't last very long. Yet they produce for us a glory that vastly outweighs them and will last forever! So we don't look at the troubles we can see now; rather, we fix our gaze on things that cannot be seen. For the things we see now will soon be gone, but the things we cannot see will last forever.

2 CORINTHIANS 4:16-18

For everything there is a season, a time for every activity under heaven. A time to be born and a time to die. A time to plant and a time to harvest. A time to kill and a time to heal. A time to tear down and a time to build up. A time to cry and a time to laugh. A time to grieve and a time to dance. A time to scatter stones and a time to gather stones. A time to embrace and a time to turn away. A time to search and a time to quit searching. A time to keep and a time to throw away. A time to tear and a time to mend. A time to be quiet and a time to speak. A time to love and a time to hate. A time for war and a time for peace. What do people really get for all their hard work? I have seen the burden God has placed on us all. Yet God has made everything beautiful for its own time. He has planted eternity in the human heart, but even so, people cannot see the whole scope of God's work from beginning to end.

ECCLESIASTES 3:1-11

stop, reflect & release

What emotions/feelings do I need to identify to begin processing them?

Do I need additional resources or support during this season of my life?

What resources are available to me? What is my plan to access them?

draw near

Heavenly Father, thank you for the gift of Your Son, Jesus, who can sympathize with us in the depths of our emotions. Help us to recognize and process our emotions so that what we are feeling remains a fact but does not become the truth that we live by. Help us to trust that Your word is true and that this season will come to an end. Show us the resources You have placed around us and remind us that despair won't last always.

In Jesus' Name, Amen.

resources

988 Suicide & Crisis Lifeline | Call 988
National Alliance on Mental Illness HelpLine | 800.950.NAMI (6264)
Cleveland Clinic | https://health.clevelandclinic.org/how-to-heal-from-trauma

HAVE NO FEAR

Let's go ahead and talk about the elephant in the room. At the beginning of the divorce process, there is some degree of fear that sets in:

- Fear of how we will take care of our children and the impact this will have on their lives
- Fear of where we will live and how we will manage the new set of independent responsibilities
- Fear of how much an attorney and court fees may cost
- Fear of what retirement will look like
- Fear of feeling broken forever
- Fear that the pain will never end
- Fear of never finding love again
- Fear of judgment or other's opinions

This fear comes because we have been thrust into a flight, fight, or freeze mode to survive the onslaught of questions regarding the unknowns we must now consider and the sheer impact of our marriage ending. It is a lot to process at once.

Can I share a secret with you? This is an appropriate response, and it is okay. Fear is an embedded emotion that helps us identify potential threats. This circumstance of divorce may have awakened this feeling of fear. This feeling could also be a response to something divorce has triggered, such as a fear of lack that you've previously experienced or the anticipation of conflict that you must now address.

You may be coming out of an abusive situation or have struggled to face each day to this point. Either way, you have experienced trauma that can have a lasting impact if not addressed at the proper time and in the proper way. The only true way we can move forward is to surrender this fear to God and regain our ability to trust Him again fully.

recognizing fear

Fear can manifest in a variety of different ways. Some signs you may recognize are feeling dizzy, overwhelmed, out of control, panic, inability to eat, nausea, and a myriad of other physical and mental presentations. For me, fear emerged in the form of indecisiveness, even with the smallest decision, and spiraled into overwhelming panic and anxiety and a complete and total loss of appetite. Even my go-to favorite meals were unappealing and flavorless.

The tricky thing about fear is that it is an essential tool that helps us be aware of and avoid threats, but when our fear switch is in overdrive, we become suspicious, fearful, and unable to trust people or God. We are often paralyzed by fear instead of becoming empowered by it. Identifying what events or conversations trigger your fear response is essential. Is it when your former spouse has their custodial weekend? Is it when you receive a text or phone call regarding court proceedings? Or maybe it's the silent time between interactions where intrusive thoughts become dominant thoughts to make you so fearful of the future that you can't see the small victories of today.

fear isn't welcome anymore

As the initial shock begins to settle, one key decision you must make moving forward is this: FEAR IS NOT WELCOME HERE ANYMORE! We must choose to operate from a place of wisdom. We must choose to make informed decisions and not be paralyzed by fear of the unknown or the final outcome of this season of our lives. We will gain our strength from the Lord, and we will renew our minds (Romans 12:2) with who Scripture says we are and what Scripture says we can do! This process is a spiritual and mental fight that takes a daily decision to place your life in the hands of a capable God and allow Him to keep your heart and mind at peace.

The enemy's only goal is to enter our lives to kill, steal, or destroy. The way Jesus defeated the enemy was not by speaking what he heard or sharing a catchy meme. No! He used the word of God to defeat the enemy (Matthew 4:1-11). We must decide very early in this battle to suit up and find weapons of war and remind ourselves that even though we are feeling everything in this fleshly body, this battle is spiritual — and we will win!

sure ground

Don't be afraid, for I am with you. Don't be discouraged, for I am your God. I will strengthen you and help you. I will hold you up with my victorious right hand.

ISAIAH 41:10

For God has not given us a spirit of fear and timidity, but of power, love, and self-discipline.

2 TIMOTHY 1:7

Such love has no fear, because perfect love expels all fear. If we are afraid, it is for fear of punishment, and this shows that we have not fully experienced his perfect love.

1 JOHN 4:18

I prayed to the LORD, and he answered me. He freed me from all my fears.

PSALM 34:4

This is my command—be strong and courageous! Do not be afraid or discouraged. For the LORD your God is with you wherever you go.

JOSHUA 1:9

Fearing people is a dangerous trap, but trusting the LORD means safety.

PROVERBS 29:25

stop, reflect & release

How is fear manifesting in your life?

How can you harness fear and use it as motivation or power?

How can you release this fear in order to trust God again?

draw near

Heavenly Father, thank you for being my strength in the midst of weakness. Help me remember that in my weakness, Your strength is made perfect. Help me make wise decisions. Help me trust You again so that I find peace in Your sovereign plan. Fear has no place in my home or my life because You have not given me a spirit of fear but of power and love and a sound mind. As I seek You, You will keep me in perfect peace.

In Jesus' Name, Amen.

FEAR IS NOT WELCOME HERE ANYMORE!

TRUST YOURSELF

While dealing with divorce, you will question your decision-making. When you think you've spent enough time with someone to know them and find out you were wrong, you will doubt yourself, your discernment, your ability to see, and your ability to make decisions.

During the divorce process and even afterward, trusting your own decision-making is like walking on a practice tightrope. The practice tightrope is approximately a foot or two off the ground. The performer typically practices gaining their balance on this lower rope, allowing them to practice while looking before putting on the blindfold. They continue to practice on the lower rope blindfolded because although they are only a couple of feet off the ground, with their vision occluded, the perceived feeling is of being on the actual tightrope. We know we are capable of making safe choices and decisions, but with our vision occluded with this recent life event, every decision feels monumental, as if we are walking on the high ropes instead of the low.

Small decisions such as buying my son gray shoes or black shoes became overwhelming — gray to me looked better, but black would match best. In reality, both would equally compliment any outfit, and he was going to rough them up at daycare anyway. Making more important decisions, such as health insurance coverage, was impossible, so I stuck with the previous plan and had to deal with the coverage and co-pay issues as they arose because I simply could not make that decision. What I'd noticed, with the help of my therapist, was that I'd taken on a lot of the responsibility and guilt of my marriage ending. My self-talk consisted of many "If I had only, then maybe..." scenarios while processing my reality. I found that I had lost trust in my decision-making and my ability to discern right from wrong or even best from better.

regaining trust

In the midst of my indecisiveness, one opportunity after another came my way. My response was along the lines of, "I'll need to process that and get back to you." If sleeping was processing, that was the only processing I did. I knew these were good opportunities, but I also knew I was in no place to make decisions about them. I began to pray that God would go before me and shut every door not meant for me during that season. Every time a door closed, I knew it was God being a very present help and directing my steps. But if the door remained open, I would walk through it confidently as prepared as possible. I didn't recognize it then, but God was slowly building my confidence in myself in what I could do and accomplish. I started telling myself, "I am capable of making decisions, and if my decision isn't the best, I will extend myself grace." When it came to smaller things like the shoes I mentioned before, I burst into laughter one day when it dawned on me to use the return policy if I purchased something that didn't work out. How simple was that? This realization gave me the confidence to move forward with my decision-making and the freedom to change my mind later. This point may seem elementary, but I was really struggling in this area. Like the tightrope walker, I wanted to learn how to gain confidence in the little things so I could move toward the more significant challenges and feel supported.

I'm thankful for the mysterious ways God moves on our behalf. During this season, God blessed me with a promotion and surrounded me with people who were highlighting all of the positive skills and qualities I possessed that I couldn't see for myself. Divorce had dealt a solid blow to my confidence, and it was as if God was saying, "You may not remember who you are, but I know and see who I've made you to be." Day by day, it felt like a bit of sun and water were applied to my heap of dirt, and in time, the seed hidden in darkness began to break through and emerge into the light.

sound check

During this season, running thoughts and ideas by our wise counsel is helpful and ensures what makes sense in our heads also makes sense when we say it out loud. They may be able to offer wisdom or see potential blessings or challenges that we have overlooked in the process of just trying to get it done. They also serve as a form of accountability to help us maintain our relationship with the Lord. Monitoring what and who we listen to during this season is vital. We must be aware that what and who we listen to can impact our thought process, welcoming confusion or peace. We need to weed out people who only feed into the negative thoughts we may be thinking because not everyone in your life will give you wise counsel. Also, listening to positive and uplifting music can have the desired effect or keep hope within our hearts, while the 90's R&B hit list will probably drop us into loneliness and tears, making us question our decisions. You have to cultivate your surroundings effectively to find solace.

Lastly, quiet time with God is also where He can begin to fine-tune our hearing. Even if we don't fully trust our decision-making, we can be confident in what He speaks when we are able to hear His voice louder than the unbelief in our hearts.

sure ground

Your word is a lamp to guide my feet and a light for my path.
PSALM 119:105

If you need wisdom, ask our generous God, and he will give it to you. He will not rebuke you for asking.
JAMES 1:5

Don't worry about anything; instead, pray about everything. Tell God what you need and thank him for all he has done.
PHILIPPIANS 4:6

stop, reflect & release

How will you rebuild confidence in trusting yourself again?

Are there outside influences that are impacting your decision-making?

Identify three people who can be a sounding board for difficult decisions.

draw near

Heavenly Father, you are my hiding place, and I can find safety and rest in You. Protect me during this time and surround me with godly influences who are able to see the best of me when I am unable to. Build my confidence in my ability to make sound decisions day by day. Show me which way I should go when I need clarification. Erase all doubts in my mind and help me learn to trust myself and, most importantly, You.

In Jesus' Name, Amen.

You may not *remember* who you are,
but I *know and see* who I've made
you to be.

GOD

VISITS FROM ANGER

The divorce process can set off an explosion of emotions. Although we won't discuss them all, anger is a topic we can't neglect. Feeling angry is not a sin. However, we have to focus on the actions that can follow our response to anger.

In the Bible, anger is typically displayed in response to sin, injustice, or false teachings. I imagine divorce could be a result of sin or injustice, which is simply defined as "unjust or unfair actions or treatment." Anger is a tricky bedfellow, one you should closely examine whenever it pops up. When injustice or sin occurs, anger can be justifiable and serve as a warning not to make the same mistake again when well-tempered.

However, unchecked anger can turn into resentment and bitterness, which can be a metastatic cancer, touching, invading, and infecting every area of our lives. It can provide a barrier of protection from repeated insults but also has the potential to insulate us from the help and healthy love that we need in this season. Most importantly, anger in our relationship with God can give space to the enemy to create division between us and Him, who can quench that fire that rages inside.

anger towards God

This topic is a taboo subject. I live somewhere in the middle of varying schools of thought. I don't want to question the sovereignty of God because He knows the end from the beginning, but I do desire a better understanding of why something I prayed for and submitted to God had a less-than-favorable outcome. I also don't see in Scripture where it is sacrilegious to feel anger when our hopes and prayers for a situation don't match the outcome God allowed. I find it silly to attempt to hide this emotion from God, knowing that He is keenly aware of how we feel anyway.

Initially, it can be hard to see how all of this can work towards bringing glory to God through the haze of emotions. Even after the dust settles, it can still be hard to understand how pain, grief, heartache, and adversity can "work together for good." It can be easy to allow our emotions to determine what we believe about God in this season. However, I encourage you to reflect on the nature and character of God you have experienced consistently in the past. Look past the anger and consider how God has proven Himself to be faithful and present.

managing anger

It can be hard to swallow the lump of anger, but you're not doing it for yourself alone. Even during this season of our lives, I'd challenge you to remember that our lives are on display for believers and unbelievers alike. I don't say this to put pressure on anyone or to minimize the difficulty of this season, but rather to remind you that even in this, it is an opportunity to bring glory to God. How will our devotion to God and ability to trust His sovereignty encourage a fellow believer to seek God with greater passion? How will your testimony of God's faithfulness encourage someone to surrender their life to Christ?

Ultimately, we have to consider: What will anger produce in us? What will anger produce out of us? Let's discuss a few ways to manage anger when it arises.

Establish Boundaries: During this season, knowing and sticking to your limits is essential! Know when to walk away from the conversation or when to put down the phone during a heated text exchange. For the sake of boundaries, it may mean it's time for you to say "No!" and stick to it. For some, sticking to your boundaries could look like learning to verbalize the time needed to process information instead of a knee-jerk emotional word salad.

Find a Healthy Outlet: Anger left unexpressed can result in physical changes that have the potential to produce illness in our bodies. Violently expressing every thought and emotion can impact the outcome of future court hearings or even custody battles. Exercising, journaling, picking up a creative hobby, or meeting with a therapist versed in divorce are a few constructive expressions.

Accept Grace: There will be days when you are surprised by how well you handled a previously challenging situation. Then, there will be days when the situation manhandles you. We want to avoid getting lost in disappointment during those tough days. Give yourself grace. Let's revisit the situation and discuss how it could have gone so we are better prepared when we face that challenge again.

Inviting God into this space allows us to be open and honest with where we are. It also makes room for Him to come and mend our broken hearts so that healing can begin. This process takes place over time and requires periodic check-ins to assess the state of our hearts and emotions. Scripture encourages us to come to God boldly, with confidence, and in truth so that we may obtain grace in our time of need. When we are able to confess our faults to God truthfully, we can access healing (James 5:16), which can permeate our personal, professional, and platonic relational lives. Just because people see our storm doesn't mean they should feel the wind and rain. Forgo living in anger and instead intentionally pursue healing for yourself and those who do life with you.

sure ground

Understand this, my dear brothers and sisters: You must all be quick to listen, slow to speak, and slow to get angry. Human anger does not produce the righteousness God desires.

JAMES 1:19-20

Fools vent their anger, but the wise quietly hold it back.

PROVERBS 29:11

God is an honest judge. He is angry with the wicked every day.

PSALMS 7:11

Don't sin by letting anger control you. Think about it overnight and remain silent.

PSALMS 4:4

stop, reflect & release

Will the fruit you bear from anger be a good example to my children on how to handle anger and disappointment?

Have you been honest with God about your anger? Why are you hiding what He already knows?

How can you invite God into this space so healing can begin?

draw near

Heavenly Father, I am angry about the outcome of my marriage. It is hard for me to understand how all of this can work together for good. I know Your ways are sovereign, so please help me find comfort in knowing Your plans for me are good and that You will never leave me nor forsake me. I surrender my anger to You so that You can work on my heart and bring about healing.

In Jesus' Name, Amen.

ANGER MAY VISIT...

DON'T LET IT MOVE IN

RESTORED FROM WITHIN

A dear family friend of mine was working on restoring her childhood home. Due to unforeseen circumstances, she was returning to a place she never anticipated living in again. Some areas would require a gut job and total renovation, and other work was more cosmetic, and although it needed to be done, it did not make the house uninhabitable.

When she began the process, there was an energy and push to get things moving and completed. As the process started, as most construction jobs do, some pauses and delays brought the pace of the project to a jog rather than a full sprint. All of the tasks became overwhelming, and it was difficult to remember that the end result, even if it was not her original plan for living, would ultimately provide a mortgage-free home with future renting potential.

This is how the process of restoration can look. We are eager and excited when something out of this divorce process finally starts to look up. It could be your case is finally moving forward with a "sell by" date; it could mean your final court hearing is on the horizon; or it could even look like finding a balanced parenting agreement that genuinely takes the child's best interest into account. Processes are happening, and things are falling into place. When we are almost ready to exhale, a delay or submission error catches us off guard.

restoration of life

I started to feel alive in my own skin again just before traveling to Atlanta for a women's retreat. This feeling came 18 months after my divorce process began and eight months after my divorce had been finalized. I could look in the mirror and recognize myself! I didn't see sadness and depression or fears and anxiety. I saw joy, hope, and healing.

Had I gone to this retreat any earlier, I would have still been in a place of high alert. I would have slept at any opportunity given, missed out on making wonderful sisterhood connections, and missed all of the beauty and splendor at the campground venue we were nestled in.

I was able to exhale all of the stress of being in survival mode and began to inhale the joy of each day. I started to find purpose in serving others and, more so, had a desire to serve others again. I saw my self-confidence reignite alongside a boldness I had lost somewhere in the past four or so years of my life. It was a time I could simply be me, and that was enough.

God truly lifted my heart and spirit to a place where I could dream and hope for future planning instead of dreading what was missing.

restoration of goods

As God began to restore the material things in my life, this took place in various ways. Buying my new bookcase and kitchen table and assembling them myself really brought me to a place of thankfulness and tears because it was symbolic of portions of my tangible life being reassembled. Restoration also came in the form of family giving me appliances they were replacing or no longer using or friends sharing gently used clothing for my son that continue to be a blessing.

We never know how God will restore until He does, but it also takes humility to accept gifts and not offer payment that you simply don't have. I would often pray for the restoration of various material things that had been lost in my divorce process. During this time, I remember reading Joel 2:25:

> The LORD says, "I will give you back what you lost to the swarming locusts, the hopping locusts, the stripping locusts, and the cutting locusts."

Now, here is the kicker! This next part is the closing line of the text that we often omit in quoting the previous phrase:

> "It was I who sent this great destroying army against you."

When I saw that last sentence, it literally took me two days to come to terms with the sovereignty of God in allowing this season of testing. It wasn't meant to destroy us or completely deplete us but to build us up in our faith and reliance on Him. In essence, God made space for Himself to show up in a grand way — not just in provision but in the restoration of not just enough but into abundance that we will not lack anymore!

restoration of love

This area can be a bit tricky to navigate. If God brings about restoration in your marriage, that is one thing. But we want to be wise in not pursuing love before its time, especially during or after the divorce process. My desire is to find a balance between being open to love being redeemed in my life and not being desperate to find a spouse. But this isn't the only way love can be redeemed.

For a while after my divorce, I would attempt to pray for my son's father, and the only thing I could sincerely offer up was, "God, he is your son. You know what he needs." I was still very hurt and offended by what had taken place, and quite honestly, I didn't want my son's father to succeed. I wanted him to be impacted as I had been impacted.

I remember the day when my prayers for my son's father had matured beyond what I mentioned before, and I truly felt the ability, but more so the willingness, to intercede on his behalf spiritually. This change is the other way that love can be restored. That is to love God enough and trust in His promises so much so we can walk in godly love and forgiveness.

This restoration does not look like opening the door to abuse or immediately accepting someone back because they apologized. This change looks like praying for your former spouse's salvation because no soul should be lost. It does not look like taking verbal abuse during conversations or text exchanges. Restored love can look like turning away from a former spouse's attempt to insight rage by calmly stating, "I hear you're upset. I'm choosing not to have this conversation in this manner because the outcome won't be beneficial. I have the next hour free – feel free to call me back when we can discuss this without yelling."

Restoration is a process with stalls and delays, setbacks, and marked progression. We have to be patient and remain open during this process, holding fast to God's word that outlines not only what He is capable of doing but also what He is willing to do in our lives through this session.

sure ground

Restore to me the joy of your salvation, and make me willing to obey you.

PSALMS 51:12

"Is this true?" the king asked her. And she told him the story. So he directed one of his officials to see that everything she had lost was restored to her, including the value of any crops that had been harvested during her absence.

2 KINGS 8:6
(CONTEXT VERSES 5-6)

In his kindness God called you to share in his eternal glory by means of Christ Jesus. So after you have suffered a little while, he will restore, support, and strengthen you, and he will place you on a firm foundation.

1 PETER 5:10

stop, reflect & release

What areas are you asking God to restore? List them out specifically.

What could restoration look like in your life?

draw near

Heavenly Father, thank you for drawing my attention to Your sovereignty regarding what You have allowed in this season. Although it is painful, I trust that You will work all things together for my good and Your glory. In every area of loss or lack, I ask that You would restore in abundance so that I may be able to bless others in their time of need. Help me be patient as you walk with me through this process. And when I doubt, remind me that I can put my trust in You and Your word.

In Jesus' Name, Amen.

TRUSTING GOD'S NATURE

It can be misleading to think that, as believers, our lives will be free from sorrows or challenges and that accepting Christ gives us a cloak of invisibility to the troubles of this world. That notion couldn't be further from the truth. We live in a fallen world where sickness, depravity, and evil run rampant. While salvation in Christ offers us a promise and hope to spend eternity with our Heavenly Father, free from the punishment we deserve, it does not end suffering in this world. This is why bad things can happen to good people.

As we face challenging situations, we tend to equate our negative situation to our finite thinking that God mustn't like us or is punishing us for something we did or didn't do. We begin to equate God's character to our suffering. "Character" can be defined as "the aggregate of features and traits that form the individual nature of some person or thing." When we talk about the different characteristics of God, we are putting vocabulary to the nature, the elements, and attributes that define who He is.

When I charge into a conversation with God, full of hot and fiery emotions, I can imagine Him giving me a double take, a bit of a side eye, yet patiently waiting for me to finish. As I calm down, I imagine a grand throat clear taking place and God squaring up to rehearse His track record in my life, much like He did Job:

> Then the Lord answered Job from the whirlwind: "Who is this that questions my wisdom with such ignorant words? Brace yourself like a man, because I have some questions for you, and you must answer them. "Where were you when I laid the foundations of the earth? Tell me, if you know so much. Who determined its dimensions and stretched out the surveying line? What supports its foundations, and who laid its cornerstone as the morning stars sang together and all the angels shouted for joy? Who kept the sea inside its boundaries as it burst from the womb, and as I clothed it with clouds and wrapped it in thick darkness? For I locked it behind barred gates, limiting its shores. I said, 'This far and no farther will you come. Here your proud waves must stop!'"
>
> **JOB 38:1-11**

I, in turn, come back with my pride humbled and my heart softened, responding as Job did:

> Then Job replied to the Lord: "I know that you can do anything, and no one can stop you. You asked, 'Who is this that questions my wisdom with such ignorance?' It is I—and I was talking about things I knew nothing about, things far too wonderful for me. You said, 'Listen and I will speak! I have some questions for you, and you must answer them.' I had only heard about you before, but now I have seen you with my own eyes. I take back everything I said, and I sit in

dust and ashes to show my repentance."

JOB 42:1-6

We aren't in a position to tell God how to make His glory visible in our lives. We are in a position to pause and take time to see how God has proven Himself by displaying various features of His character. I often find that challenging seasons present a grand opportunity for God to display another characteristic of Himself.

character of god

We learn about the character and nature of God by reading and studying our Bibles. In this, we begin to hear the voice, the rhythm, of God in a way that when the enemy attempts to lead us astray with negative thoughts, we can recognize and say, "That doesn't sound like God." How we move from knowledge of His character to experiencing His character typically comes in some form of challenge – seeking peace, wisdom, instruction, healing, or provision, for example. In experiencing the character of God, we can speak from a personal encounter of His glory being displayed in our lives. Here are a few characteristics of God:

- **God is patient.** He is patient in our learning and in our mistakes. *See Nehemiah 9:17.*

- **God is reliable.** His love or concern does not change based on our attitudes or situations. We can always count on Him to be present in our circumstances when we call on Him. *See Hebrews 13:8.*

- **God is a provider.** He meets our needs. Maybe not everything we want, but He will ensure that our essential needs are met. *See Matthew 6:26.*

Listen, there were some months during and even after my divorce proceedings that I genuinely have no clue how all the bills were paid because the math was not mathing! I picked up a side job partly to pass the time of being away from my son but also because I was afraid of not having enough. One night, my eyes filled with tears as I pleaded with God to make Himself visible in this situation. Initially, my tears were based on fear of not knowing how this situation would work out. But by the end of my prayer, my tears were full of rejoicing because I had experienced, in the past and present, the faithfulness and goodness of God.

The seasoned believers would say: "Trust God when you can't trace Him." While walking through divorce, there are days when His presence may be pervasive, and there are other days where tracing His presence is likened to dropping a rock in a deep well – you may not hear the pebble hit the bottom, and if you do, the sound is faint. When you have experienced something so sweet, all you want to do is tell others. This book is a form of testimony that speaks like Scripture, saying, "Taste and see that the Lord is good..." (Psalms 34:8). I've tasted the goodness of the Lord, and I've seen it, too. I hope you have the same opportunity to see God's character and better understand His will for you.

sure ground

God is not a man, so he does not lie. He is not human, so he does not change his mind. Has he ever spoken and failed to act? Has he ever promised and not carried it through?

NUMBER 23:19

Then let the heavens proclaim his justice, for God himself will be the judge.

PSALMS 50:6

For the Lord God is our sun and our shield. He gives us grace and glory. The Lord will withhold no good thing from those who do what is right. O Lord of Heaven's Armies, what joy for those who trust in you.

PSALMS 84:11-12

stop, reflect & release

In the past, what characteristics of God have you seen displayed in your life?

In this current season, what characteristics of God are present?

How is it possible for God to remain good even in trying situations?

draw near

Heavenly Father, thank you for being present amid this challenge. Continue to remind me of Your faithfulness, as You have proven Yourself time and time again. Help me remember that the quality of my circumstances does not affect the character of who You are. Show me what part of Your nature You're creating space for in my life. During each season, help me see what portion of Your nature is on display. I trust that You are good and Your plans for me are good even in challenging situations.

In Jesus' Name, Amen.

GETTING UNTANGLED

For a plant to grow to its full potential, it requires selective pruning of dead, infected, or injured leaves. Without pruning, life is drained from the healthy portion of the plant as it tries to help and heal the ailing areas. If pruning doesn't occur, the plant will begin to die, and disease will spread throughout the plant. This process can be a direct reflection of how our lives will start to wither and die if we remain connected to things of the past.

As we gain strength, we gradually start disconnecting from our former life, marriage, and way of doing things. This process will look a variety of ways for many people. Finding the best plan for your situation requires leaning into that safe community and closing your ears to anyone not offering wise counsel. Even with the best intentions, people can speak out of turn, and words can cut deep during such a vulnerable time. The level of disconnecting will vary based on the length of your marriage, any children produced from that marriage, and potentially the reason(s) why the marriage ended.

Nevertheless, you have two families trying to sort the pieces of who goes where and when! Based on our individual situations, there may be in-laws who never change even though your status did. They may welcome you with open arms and respectful boundaries. Others may never say hi or check on you or their grandkids, vanishing as if they never knew you or if you knew them. Where do biological children and stepchildren fit into this equation? What happens when the stepchild forms a relationship with the stepparent that transcends the divorce? All of these are difficult areas to navigate based on the complexity of each situation.

untangling your mind

I always had the mindset that each marriage should be uniquely its own. Each marriage has a distinct set of individuals becoming one. Likewise, each divorce is unique, with its own quirks along the way. You have become accustomed to considering how decisions will impact your family, and now you may be the only person impacted. Going to the grocery store and shopping for one person instead of two, or realizing you are the only grocery shopper, is something you may have to adjust to. This example is just one of a few nuances that many don't consider once the undoing is done. Your mind really needs a reboot to adjust to some of the changes.

The area of self-talk (what you say to yourself) may also need some work. Shame and guilt can cause us to get into the habit of assuming blame and taking responsibility that may not be ours. For some, abuse was a factor in the relationship. So, even though we are away from the abuser, we can still hear their taunting or defeatist statements ringing in our ears. Those of us involved with a narcissist may consider our feelings invalid or over the top after years of gaslighting. All of our stories are unique, yet all of our minds need to be disconnected from that portion of our past so we can move into the bright future ahead of us.

untangling your expectations

Coming to the realization that the person I dated and was engaged to was not the same person I married took time. We all initially present our *representative* instead of the *real us* in some shape or form to impress one another, but that isn't what I'm referring to when I say I did not marry the person I dated. I'm speaking of a persona developed on a myriad of lies that, around each turn, a new personality joined the party.

I kept expecting the *representative* to show up and do all he said he would. Time after time, the empty and broken promises became the soundtrack that was living rent-free in my head. As the divorce process took its course, I continued to expect the *representative* to show up and be amicable and reasonable regarding assets and co-parenting, especially since we had discussed taking this road so things wouldn't get messy. Chile, the moral of that story is to stop putting *gallon-size* expectations on someone who is only capable of *pint-size* responsibilities.

This point isn't meant to bash anyone, but more so to say expectations can leave us in a pit of continued offense when we expect a now-former spouse to demonstrate husband-like or wife-like qualities toward us, especially during the divorce process. I honestly had to separate my emotions from who I had known and make every interaction from the mindset of a business transaction. My feelings were too closely connected to who I had known and, at times, caused me to make decisions that didn't benefit the situation.

untangling your future

Just because we were headed down a similar path with our former spouses doesn't mean we must remain on that path once our marriage ends. This space after the marriage is a time of rediscovering and redefining who we are as individuals. It could be time to take those hobbies and skills placed on the shelf and dust them off again. It may look like returning to school and finishing your degree. It could also look like fixing financial and legal issues accumulated from your former marriage so you can move forward debt-free and in peace.

Striving to heal spiritually, emotionally, physically, and financially is beneficial and necessary as we focus on what lies ahead. All things are being made new as we purposefully choose to take one step forward each day. We move forward only by untangling ourselves from the mess of the past. We will no longer be bound to our past as we connect to the true vine, God, who can provide us sustenance, rest, and abundant life. Untangle from the negative and allow yourself to be wrapped up in God's embrace to find peace moving forward.

sure ground

Don't lie to each other, for you have stripped off your old sinful nature and all its wicked deeds. Put on your new nature, and be renewed as you learn to know your Creator and become like him.

COLOSSIANS 3:9-10

We use God's mighty weapons, not worldly weapons, to knock down the strongholds of human reasoning and to destroy false arguments. We destroy every proud obstacle that keeps people from knowing God. We capture their rebellious thoughts and teach them to obey Christ.

2 CORINTHIANS 10:4-5

We can make our plans, but the Lord determines our steps.

PROVERBS 16:9

For I am about to do something new. See, I have already begun! Do you not see it? I will make a pathway through the wilderness. I will create rivers in the dry wasteland.

ISAIAH 43:19

stop, reflect & release

Are there ways you are still clinging to your former spouse or former life?

What healing connections can remain with appropriate boundaries?

What unhealthy connections need to be severed?

draw near

Heavenly Father, thank you for loving me and caring for me. Thank You for strengthening me and healing me along this process. Help me discern what areas need to be surrendered to You. Show me how to become free from the past so I can learn to live an abundant life in You. Instead of holding on to what was, help me look forward to what can be through You.

In Jesus' Name, Amen.

PAIN AND HEARTACHE

There aren't words to describe the physical and emotional pain felt during a divorce. Nothing compares to the pain of someone you were willing to submit your life to coming along and upending your life. Tears are the only currency of exchange to explain the heartache felt when someone who was supposed to protect your heart ends up crushing it and attempting to grind the remaining fragments into fine dust to scatter into the wind. When the one who vowed to build you up is the main person tearing you down, the word "pain" isn't descriptive enough to help those who have never experienced divorce understand the season of life you are currently facing. The ultimate truth is that unless someone has been in this situation, they truly won't understand where you are coming from, which is okay.

I believe in being honest with our feelings and being able to really lean into the vulnerability and rawness of that moment. This act doesn't mean I set up residence, but for us to be fully healed in time to come, it only makes sense that we bring all of our hurt and the fullness of our hurt to a God who already knows the depths of what we are feeling. Why should we attempt to hide or minimize our feelings to an omnipotent God?

how to respond to pain

I can empathize with the pain and heartbreak Job felt after his family's death, the loss of his possessions, illness, and friends who continued to blame him for his life's state. Even during his trials, Job remained faithful to God. Even though he lost what seemingly mattered most to him, Job stood firm on his eternal hope, and in time, it was all restored.

I can empathize with the pain and heartbreak of Leah doing everything within her power to serve and submit to her husband, yet her husband loved and favored her sister more. I can imagine the rejection that she felt as she questioned her value and worth. Yet, God restored her value by opening her womb to bless her with children, which was of significant importance in her time. Leah was able to bear children while her sister's womb remained closed. Leah relied on the faithfulness of God to mend the space between her and her husband. As a result of her trust and faithfulness to God, she was able to live in the land of inheritance with her husband by her side.

I can empathize with Ruth and Naomi as they lost everything following the deaths of their husbands. In their honesty and humility, they moved from one season of asking to gather from one corner of the field to becoming owners of the field in another season. These figures are examples of people who experienced profound loss in various ways yet remained faithful to God and saw restoration by His hand. In reading these stories in the Bible, I find comfort in knowing I'm not the only one who has experienced a deep hurt. I am further comforted by their testimony of faith as they stood during challenging seasons.

healing is here

There is a saying that says, "Time heals all wounds." I believe time allows us to process the events of our lives from a more rational rather than emotional place. With time, the wounds turn into scabs that eventually do heal, yet they leave scars. Scars remind us of where we've been, what we've experienced, and what we've made it through. I would argue that time spent with God heals all wounds. Luke 4:18-19 says:

> The Spirit of the Lord is upon me, for he has anointed me to bring Good News to the poor. He has sent me to proclaim that captives will be released, that the blind will see, that the oppressed will be set free, and that the time of the Lord's favor has come.

It is such a comfort to me to be able to find a scripture that speaks directly to where I am in this season. I am, we are, the "brokenhearted" — those whose hearts have been broken due to situations we have faced in this world. Jesus Christ was sent specifically to heal us and free us from the weight of this disappointment. Divorce may seem minor to others, but it has been an event with a major impact on our lives, and Christ cares about that and me! He doesn't want me to remain crushed or oppressed —He is near and comes to heal me and set me free. This season will have its challenges, and the going may get tough before it gets better. However, I am assured that if we continue to rely on God and allow Christ through the power of the Holy Spirit to work within us, there will be a day when we, too, will be able to share the good news so that others may be healed, set free, and able to regain sight not only of who they are but also of who Christ is.

sure ground

The Lord is close to the brokenhearted; he rescues those whose spirits are crushed. The righteous person faces many troubles, but the Lord comes to the rescue each time.
PSALMS 34:18-19

He heals the brokenhearted and bandages their wounds.
PSALMS 147:3

This High Priest of ours understands our weaknesses, for he faced all of the same testings we do, yet he did not sin.
So let us come boldly to the throne of our gracious God. There we will receive his mercy, and we will find grace to help us when we need it most.
HEBREWS 4:15-16

stop, reflect & release

Take time to reflect and write your honest emotions and what they are tied to.

Even amid pain and heartbreak, how has Christ felt near to you?

What can it look like to be healed from heartbreak, set free, and regain sight?

draw near

Heavenly Father, thank you for caring enough about me and this season of life where Jesus Christ was sent to meet my needs. Thank you for recognizing and understanding the impact this has had on my life and the pain disappointment has caused. Help me remain faithful in this season and open to Christ healing and restoring me. Help me trust in You, as You are not like man and will not lie. Help me learn how to honor you in this season.

In Jesus' Name, Amen.

YOU CAN'T HIDE
YOUR FEELINGS
FROM AN OMNIPOTENT GOD

YOU NEED A VILLAGE

During the initial stages of this season and possibly for quite some time after, we can find ourselves in extremely vulnerable states. We can find ourselves seeking comfort and security in places or things. This stage can be a time when people turn to old vices and habits. Self-awareness and reflection may be a challenge while tackling everything else, so having a safe place with safe people to be in community with is essential!

Unfortunately, those people and spaces aren't often found in brick-and-mortar church buildings. People going through a divorce, especially within local assemblies, have found a void of safe spaces and, specifically, community to be able to process and find strength and safety. There's typically a small group for wives, mothers (consisting of married women), singles, and men's groups (typically single or married men), but where do the divorced individuals go to gain strength? Perhaps through divine intervention or possibly the algorithms of technology, but my safe community arrived via Facebook in 2023! A true godsend was locating a Divorce Care group at a local church. This church facilitated a 14-week program that allowed us to speak honestly regarding our processes but constantly challenged us to remain in right standing with God, which can be challenging when you want to tell your former spouse why, where, and what for! This group gave me perspective and reminded me that I was not alone. My group consisted of people of all ethnicities, varying ages, and a wide range of lengths and qualities of marriage. Sharing our trials and triumphs bonded us together in a supernatural way. We were able to draw strength from one another, offer suggestions, and provide insight to others for what was to come based on where everyone was in their process.

stay connected

The Bible has a parable about a lost sheep (Mark 18:10-14, Luke 15:1-7). In that parable, Jesus speaks of the shepherd leaving the ninety-nine in search of the one lost sheep. I want to focus on two portions of that text:

- **THE NINETY-NINE** For the shepherd to leave in search of the lost sheep, he had to ensure the flock's safety. We cannot ignore how much this speaks to the power of a healthy community and the care of a good shepherd to ensure that we are secured in a safe place.

- **THE ONE** There is no way to overlook that the shepherd was concerned enough about the one missing sheep to ensure the flock was safe and then go in search of the one. What an amazing display of love and concern! Every single soul matters to God. He will not leave you in this season because He is concerned that we remain in the fold.

It doesn't matter if you choose to join a Divorce Care group or if you find 2-3 trustworthy friends who can hold your conversations close to their hearts and the ear of God, who can pray with you, and who can sit in non-judgmental silence as you share this portion of your journey — you must find community!

In the parable mentioned before, another visual also comes to mind. I imagine the small lost sheep was oblivious to the potential danger surrounding it. I see the wolves recognizing a vulnerable sheep separated, moving independently, from its shepherd. Like the opportunist they are, the wolves begin to stalk the sheep, sometimes for hours, to insight a baseline level of nervousness or fear and wear down their potential prey. Once the wolves see signs of weakness and fatigue, they have a planned attack for the fastest wolves to cause the prey to dart and run to expend their last remaining bits of energy before the power wolves come in to deliver more fatal blows. Does this sound familiar?

Sometimes, we experience a difficult situation in life that may limit our prayer or devotional time with the Lord. From there, our attitude towards God and the church body may become more pessimistic. After a few weeks, we may decide we aren't attending church locally or online to give ourselves "space and time." Shortly after that, another life situation may hit which, in our already weakened and vulnerable state, we consider returning to heavy consumption of alcohol or just disconnecting from all who will help us keep a stable mind. Before we know it, we have wandered so far so fast that we aren't sure how to get back to safety.

We are like sheep during this time, and the enemy is an opportunistic wolf planning his attack. In loneliness and seclusion, we are perfect prey and indefensible to attacks. But because our Great Shepherd loves us and is so concerned about every single one of us, He remains in pursuit of us. He is well-equipped to keep us from harm, and one of the tools He uses is community. Find those with whom you can *do life*; find your flock. You need people who will tell you if you have salad in your teeth through a text or with a silent gesture rather than yell it across the table. We are all safer in community.

trauma bonds

I want to end this conversation by discussing trauma bonds. These bonds occur when you and another, old or new, acquaintance form a genuine connection over traumatic events. We can initially find comfort in discussing similar challenges and difficulties. However, there is a danger in creating a bond over traumatic situations because you can become stuck in a negative space. Here are ways to recognize you are trauma-bonded:

- You can only talk about negative situations regarding your circumstances.
- The only time you typically talk is to rehash past negative experiences or discuss new experiences that relate to the original traumas.
- You and the other party are unwilling, maybe even unable, to find positivity or hope that will move you forward to healing.

If you find that you've developed a trauma bond, try to address it gently but directly. When I found myself slipping into a trauma bond, I asked the other person to attend a different event that provided an opportunity for us to find commonality in other ways. She initially was agreeable but later said something had come up as she gave me a bracelet that related right back to the original traumatic conversation. She was well-intending, I know, but simply unable to move forward.

Scripture says that God is able to give us beauty for ashes. With God's help, we are capable of leaving this season's destruction to pursue and find hope, joy, and peace again. Through a safe community, our lives will see beauty again as we move forward in healing!

sure ground

> A friend is always loyal, and a brother is born to help in time of need.
>
> **PROVERBS 17:17**

> As iron sharpens iron, so a friend sharpens a friend.
>
> **PROVERBS 27:17**

> Fools think their own way is right, but the wise listen to others.
>
> **PROVERBS 12:15**

Without wise leadership a nation falls; there is safety in having many advisers.

PROVERBS 11:14

stop, reflect & release

What qualities should we look for in a safe space/safe community?

Identify your safe space/safe community.

Do you typically retreat from your community during challenging times?

How can you push yourself to remain connected?

draw near

Heavenly Father, thank you for never leaving me. Help me find a safe community of wise counsel. Surround me with a community that will check on me and encourage me during this season. Help me remain connected and not withdraw within myself. Give me wisdom and discernment of people's intentions while I am in a vulnerable state. Cover and protect me during this healing process.

In Jesus' Name, Amen.

IN PURSUIT OF PEACE

Scripture says that we should pursue peace with all men (Hebrews 12:14, Romans 12:18), and that same Scripture calls for us to "work at living a holy life." In this context, "holy" means to be separate or consecrated to the work of God. I say this to you as it was given to me: Just because we are going through a tumultuous season doesn't mean we get to lay down our confession as a believer and "act a fool," as my family would say.

In suffering, we are still responsible for laying our life down so that we may walk in the life we now have in Christ. This works in two ways. The first would be as a call to maintain your integrity, dignity, and faith walk — not perfection, but seeking His will in what you should say and do. Secondly, it serves as a reminder that we are walking out and living out this affliction, but we will do so from the mindset of and hope in Jesus Christ.

Throughout the process of divorce, I quickly found out that many things can or will be out of my control.

The narrative that the former spouse gives their circle. The people your child may be around when sharing custodial time. The outcome of mediations or hearings. What people will think when they find out. If the kids brushed their teeth twice a day or not at all. If the child support is submitted on time. When and if homework is done. Before you know it, your mind will be spinning and swirling in so many directions you can't tell up from down or going from coming.

Living our life caught up in the words of those around us will have us flustered and conflicted. However, living our life in Christ will have us warring from a place of victory and strength. If our confession of faith is tested, will we be found striving to have the last say, or will we be found praying for the best outcome, moving in wisdom? Being tossed by every wind, and there will be many, especially if your divorce involves children, that comes with the storm will leave us as castaways on an island: disoriented, desperate, and dehydrated.

peace with (wo)man

During the litigation process, the goal is to find a reasonable outcome that both parties can agree on. Things may not be fair or perfect, but they should be reasonable and not leave you with buyer's remorse. Agreeably, this may be a difficult task, but we must hold fast to our beliefs, advocate for the best possible outcome, and trust God in the entire process.

For me, this looked like a parenting plan that brought as much consistency for my son as possible yet allowed time for him to be with his father as well. Strained communication lived where I'd hoped co-parenting would exist. Like Moses' mother, Jochebed, I had to trust God and step back. When others are involved, we are simply responsible for pursuing peace, not forcing it. If it isn't received, shake off the dust and keep moving.

peace with self

This part is where we get to lift the guilt and shame we are carrying. This is where we get to find contentment as the dust settles. Knowing that I had tried everything within my strength to maintain our marriage and end things amicably when it was over brought peace to my heart. I didn't like where my life was, but after reflection and consideration, I recognized we still had our health, provisions, and life. This realization brought many things into perspective.

Things were not *perfect*, but they were *okay*, and I resolved that I/we would be okay even in less preferred situations. I didn't run into another relationship to quench the desire for companionship. I extended myself a space of grace to make mistakes and time to heal during this process. I found peace in myself during this stage, creating a better mindset.

peace with god

As I mentioned at the beginning of this chapter, we want to be in good standing with God even during this process. Maintaining an open relationship with the Lord will be the gateway to healing, contentment, and peace. We must keep our focus on God, and by doing that, He promised to keep us in perfect peace (Isaiah 26:3) and give us a peace that surpasses all of our understanding (Philippians 4:7). Which means there will be moments where we look at our situation and wonder, how am I so calm? That is God's peace!

This peace wasn't something that happened overnight for me. This process took intentionality, especially on difficult days, like holidays, after repeated offenses, heated legal battles, etc. My desire was to be whole after this process, so my focus was maintaining a healthy thought life and finding true peace, where I was no longer at war with my situation and could maintain my freedom by not being bound to the circumstances of my situation.

At the end of this season of life, we want to be able to say, "It is well." Things may not be perfect, but I hope that you can find yourself in a space of peace that is reminiscent of the lyrics of the hymn, "It Is Well," by Audrey Assad. Let God's peace flow like a river, and He will make all well.

sure ground

Then you will experience God's peace, which exceeds anything we can understand. His peace will guard your hearts and minds as you live in Christ Jesus.

PHILIPPIANS 4:7

You will keep in perfect peace all who trust in you, all whose thoughts are fixed on you!

ISAIAH 26:3

I am leaving you with a gift—peace of mind and heart. And the peace I give is a gift the world cannot give. So don't be troubled or afraid.

JOHN 14:27

In peace I will lie down and sleep, for you alone, O LORD, will keep me safe.

PSALMS 4:8

stop, reflect & release

How can you pursue peace with your former spouse?

What does finding peace with yourself look like?

What does contentment look like in this season?

draw near

Heavenly Father, thank you for giving me peace that the world cannot take away. Help me find contentment in this season, knowing that it may not be what I desire it to be, but it can still be well with me. Help me access the gift of peace through the Holy Spirit so I can pursue peace with others and find peace and rest for my soul. Draw my attention to areas that are out of my control so that I may surrender them to You in prayer. Guard my heart and mind in peace through Christ Jesus.

In Jesus' Name, Amen.

IT IS WELL

YOU WIN SOME, YOU LEARN SOME

During marriage and certainly during the divorce process, there should be lessons that we learn along the way. Scripture suggests that spouses live with each other "according to knowledge," meaning we should learn how our spouse operates. Consider things like: Are they a morning person? Do they need time to process major decisions? How do they communicate during stress? All of these things help to inform us when we would bring up difficult conversations, how early to engage them in conversation, and how much space to provide for processing.

In this season, all of those lessons still apply. How you use that wisdom in engaging in additional conversations should be evident, such as discussing business dealings or even custody agreements. These experiences can also inform our current professional, familial, or platonic relationships. Learning the rhythm of our bosses can help us navigate when to request a raise or bring up a challenging topic. It can provide insight into how to interact with our kids — do they need more space or physical touch to fill their love bucket? These lessons have value in every aspect of life when interacting with others. Some lessons don't show up until the end — *if reflection and maturity occur amongst both parties.* If not, that, too, is a lesson to be learned. Removing or lowering expectations can be a lesson that begins to protect your heart from frequent disappointment. Wisdom could look like making a phone call to discuss a challenge rather than starting a text war. In all our getting, we are encouraged to get an *understanding* — in love, life, and all relationships to encourage positive and efficient communication.

no wins are guaranteed

As my marriage began to unravel, I felt this deep sense of heaviness that I had failed — failed my marriage, my family, my son, and myself. As proceedings took place and our lives were put on display, I felt embarrassed by my decision-making and how each choice had led to the ultimate demise. Having a competitive nature, coming from a competitive sport and family, I chucked it up as a major L in my life.

In sports, the loss for me would equate to not being adequately prepared for my opponent. After a loss, an athlete or team typically reviews the statistics to see where errors were made, where performance may not have been optimal, and if the scouting report had been accurately presented and followed. Viewing the divorce from this perspective left me wondering if I had invested enough in my marriage, if I had prayed hard enough, or if

I should have taken additional time to learn more about my spouse before and during the marriage.

Even with the best scouting report and preparation, sometimes you just face extraordinary teams on their best night, and there isn't much that can be done to keep them from winning. That has been my resolve. I did all I could physically, emotionally, mentally, and spiritually to prepare for this journey; however, the adversary was firing on all cylinders, and divorce was the result.

Even with taking time to know your spouse before marriage, serving and submitting to your spouse, and being that godly husband or wife, people still have the ability to make choices and decisions outside of the will of God and according to their own free will. God will not hold someone hostage in a marriage who doesn't want to be there. God can work on a willing heart. But one that resists God, no matter how much we pray or fast, that individual must ultimately decide to humble themselves, repent, and seek change.

life lessons

All is not lost during seasons where your judgment is challenged. One thing I appreciate about God is that He is always gracious and merciful, even when we walk ourselves into danger. He allows us to learn from situations we find ourselves in, whether by our doing or someone else's. Even when things seem dire, God ensures that the lessons in life are not losses. Even in learning, we still win.

During my divorce and even after, I've asked questions like, "How did God know this would happen, and what has He planned for me in this situation? If my marriage had been restored, did He also have a plan for that?" The lessons did not immediately come to me, leaving me pondering the meaning of everything I was going through. Some lessons take time but eventually reveal themselves. The mysteries of God are far greater than I can understand. Just as a plant has various root systems that help it gain nutrients, so do the ways of God. He has a *root system*, if you will, that routes every plan and even every event in our lives and ultimately connects us back to the main source. For, in Him alone, we can live, move, and have our being. For every track our life course may run, there are lessons available if we keep our hearts softened to the voice of God.

God's character is one of love, compassion, and grace. The lessons aren't meant to sound like the crack of a whip bringing us back in line with fear. Instead, they are more like bumpers on the bowling alley lanes that gently, sometimes firmly, guide us back to the main path. The lesson may be how to decipher our plans from the will of God. Or possibly how to be sensitive to discernment. Perhaps the lesson is how to place our joy and trust in Christ. All in all, whether the outcome is preferable or not, we still win.

sure ground

"For I know the plans I have for you," says the LORD. "They are plans for good and not for disaster, to give you a future and a hope."

JEREMIAH 29:11

The Lord leads with unfailing love and faithfulness all who keep his covenant and obey his demands.

PSALMS 25:10

But God is so rich in mercy, and he loved us so much, that even though we were dead because of our sins, he gave us life when he raised Christ from the dead. (It is only by God's grace that you have been saved!)

EPHESIANS 2:4-5

stop, reflect & release

What lessons have you learned during your marriage and the divorce process?

How can you shift your perspective from seeing this as a *losing* season to a *winning* season?

What future wins would you like to achieve?

draw near

Heavenly Father, thank you for allowing us to walk through this season victoriously, knowing we will always prosper in You. Help me see the possibility for growth in the season from Your perspective. I release the embarrassment and shame of what can be defined as a failure. I receive the grace and compassion that You freely give during this course correction. Help me see the lessons this season of life will bring.

In Jesus' Name, Amen.

LESSONS NOT LOSSES

REMAINING PRESENT

My grandmother was notorious for paraphrasing or misquoting various poems, yet she would present them as the original works. My favorite was her paraphrasing of the introductory stanza of a poem by Ella Wheeler Wilcox: "Laugh, and the world laughs with you. Weep, and you weep alone. For this old world is a cruel old world and has many troubles of its own." The original text reads as follows:

> Laugh, and the world laughs with you;
> Weep, and you weep alone.
> For the sad old earth must borrow its mirth,
> But has trouble enough of its own.

When my grandmother would recite her version of the poem, it made me think of the Scripture that suggests that we focus solely on today and its troubles and not to borrow any additional troubles from tomorrow (Matthew 6:34). Yet, I found myself borrowing a lifetime worth of troubles each day. My focus was poor, my memory was shaky at best, and I didn't recognize my own reflection. The glimmer from my eyes faded as I was swept away by worry, lost in tomorrow's troubles.

remaining present for self

Remaining present first applied to myself. My sleeping habits deteriorated, my eating habits mimicked my toddler's, and exercise was a foreign language. I would comment on my low energy and lack of motivation, but I hadn't snapped into the reality of what I was doing to my body. After starting therapy, I slowly began to bring myself back into focus by making conscious choices that would impact my health in the future and, more importantly, would improve my quality of life now, giving me energy and increasing my focus overall.

There are some periods of time that are just a blur. When my divorce began, I was so busy trying to hold everything together for us and figuring out how to be a new mom while managing attorney fees, court dates, and custody schedules. All of this had me in an out-of-body experience, something similar to when the laughing gas at the dentist hits just right. I could do the motions of everyday life, but I was detached from my feelings and emotions.

I also noticed that it was challenging for me to focus on work tasks because I was so consumed by what was happening in my personal life. In seeing how my mental and emotional struggles were spilling into every aspect of my life, I realized I had to change. I began meeting with my primary care doctor, meeting regularly with my counselor, and focusing on Scripture that addressed worry and a stable mind. I recognized if I was going to be worth anything as a mother, coworker, or friend, I had to make sure I took care of myself first in order to be equipped to serve those around me.

remaining present for others

My present thoughts and energy were being consumed by fears of things to come or hypothetical scenarios that may never happen. Because I had a toddler, much of my thoughts consisted of how I would handle time away from him when I had literally been present every day of his life. But those questions were distracting me from being present in special moments, moments where we pretended to wear bowls on our heads as hats and read his favorite books over and over again. I had to make a conscious effort to keep my thoughts and focus on what was happening right in front of me and hand the future over to God. Worrying about our future was stealing the joy of what was happening right before me in the lives of those I care about.

I began to cherish each moment, knowing that my time during holidays, birthdays, and summers would be limited. It taught me to maximize each moment and not to wait or put off something I wanted to do or say because we wouldn't have that exact moment ever again. It was a blessing in disguise because it also caused me to enjoy each moment by relaxing and not stressing about whether or not it was perfect. The fact that we were having fun and making memories became the most important focus.

God of past, present, and future

Who was I fooling, thinking I could take on all the concerns of my life? As each dreaded event approached, it was reassuring and strengthening to my faith walk to see how God had gone ahead and made preparations before me. We serve a God who was present before time began and will remain once time ceases. How small-minded of me to think He would not be present here, there, and in times to come? This season has not surprised God, and just as He has done in the past, He will continue to remain a present help in our time of need, now and in the future. I'll leave you with something my uncle would always say to me:

> *"The past has passed. That's why it is behind you. The future is ahead, but too far to see in front of you. Do you know what the best gift is? Right now! That's why they call it the present. And who do you know that receives a 'present' and doesn't open it? So, don't spend too much time looking behind you or ahead of you because you will miss the gift right in front of you — the present."*

So, I encourage you to unwrap the gift of the present that's right in front of you! Be present for yourself by taking the time to take care of yourself or sign up for therapy. Be present for others by making a special picnic dinner with your child to hear about their day or by calling that friend and attentively listening instead of zoning out. Lastly, trust God, who is the author and finisher of our faith and also our lives. Visualize yourself laying every care and concern at His feet, leaving every burden in His caring hands.

sure ground

So don't worry about tomorrow, for tomorrow will bring its own worries. Today's trouble is enough for today.

MATTHEW 6:34

Do not be afraid or discouraged, for the LORD will personally go ahead of you. He will be with you; he will neither fail you nor abandon you.

DEUTERONOMY 31:8

Don't be afraid, for I am with you. Don't be discouraged, for I am your God. I will strengthen you and help you. I will hold you up with my victorious right hand.

ISAIAH 41:10

The Lord himself will fight for you. Just stay calm.

EXODUS 14:14

stop, reflect & release

What are signs that you may be distracted by future thoughts or concerns?

Identify two tasks you can complete today that impact your immediate situation.

How will you make a conscious effort to remain in the present?

draw near

Heavenly Father, thank you for always being present, going before me, and preparing the path that I will take. I apologize for not fully trusting You with my future and attempting to take matters into my own hands. When I begin to worry, remind me of Your faithfulness. Help me take each day, which is the daily bread that You have provided, as more than enough. Draw my attention to how my thoughts can wander and help me submit them back to You.

In Jesus' Name, Amen.

READY, SET, HEAL!

My experience with divorce could be described as a deep wound to the heart. Wounds heal with time and form some type of scab; if the injured area around it keeps healing, it will eventually become a scar. The process of healing, unfortunately, isn't linear. It is a process wherein some stages take longer than others, and the environment must remain healthy for the process to be completed without delay. Changes in the environment can not only delay healing but can become a breeding ground for infection or decay.

process of healing

When I speak of wounds or injuries healing physically in this chapter, I am comparing that to the process we must experience as we begin this healing journey. Leaving our hearts in a state of stress can literally result in what is medically called "Broken Heart Syndrome," where the heart is weakened after profound emotional or physical stress. Although this is and will be a difficult season, we must resolve to seek healing and wholeness first for ourselves and secondly, so we can healthily care for those around us.

1. **Stop The Bleeding** For any wound to heal, you must stop the bleeding. This may look like completing the divorce process. If advisable, this may look like moving out during the divorce process. With my former spouse refusing to move out, for me, this looked like moving the king bed out of the master bedroom and moving my old queen furniture set into the master bedroom. This new set-up became my safe place and my place of peace. It also looked like establishing boundaries of communication and allowing myself to disengage when someone crossed those boundaries.

2. **Manage Inflammation** During this process, the blood vessels expand to bring the perfect balance of oxygenated blood to clean the wound and fight off bacteria. I could liken this process to those who have finally made a clean break from an abusive situation. This could also be the person who has finally moved into their new place or even started a new job after being a homemaker for most of their married life and is in the beginning phases of establishing their "new normal."

3. **Initiate Growth and Rebuilding** Now, oxygen-rich cells begin generating new tissue. This phase is where scars start to fade. Joining a small group to get out again or even being able to talk about your process without bursting into tears would be evidence of this stage. It doesn't mean you've moved past everything that has happened, but it certainly doesn't have the

same breath-taking pain it initially had.

4. **Begin Strengthening** Over time, the tissue gets stronger and stronger, yet it never reaches its original strength. Depending on the size of the wound, this process could take weeks, months, or even years. As is true of our process, recovery takes time, and healing takes time. But both are possible!

factors that affect healing

Multiple factors can impact the rate at which healing occurs and whether the healing process happens in or out of sequence with additional interventions. Here are the areas I'd like to focus on:

Oxygen

A healthy space to heal is essential. Surrounding ourselves with those who speak life into us is vital. Putting ourselves in atmospheres of prayer and worship where God can breathe upon us is not optional. When a wound lacks adequate oxygen, the healing process is stunted, leaving a gaping hole where regeneration should have occurred.

Foreign Body

Listen, we don't need any foreign bodies, opinions, or guidance. This area speaks again to the importance of who we surround ourselves with during this season. Also, any anger, bitterness, and resentment must be released so that deep healing can take place.

Blood Supply

The blood supply is the gateway to healing. Without it, there is no possible way a wound can heal, and not only that, you are at a significant risk for infection and decay. We cannot cut off our lifeline to healing! We must remain connected to God, allowing others to pray for us and support us when needed and resolving not to give up in the midst of the storm.

Healing is not a linear journey. There can be setbacks, or some stages of healing may take longer than another stage or longer than you expect. Give yourself space and grace to naturally transition to the next phase. The goal isn't rapid results but a whole, healed heart and person. The pain of your heart may be great, even unbearable at times; however, be assured that if you continue to "lean into healing," you'll find yourself not only being healed but healed and restored by the master physician.

sure ground

Nevertheless, the time will come when I will heal Jerusalem's wounds and give it prosperity and true peace.

JEREMIAH 33:6

Then your salvation will come like the dawn, and your wounds will quickly heal. Your godliness will lead you forward, and the glory of the Lord will protect you from behind.

ISAIAH 58:8

"Lord, help!" they cried in their trouble, and he saved them from their distress. He sent out his word and healed them, snatching them from the door of death.

PSALMS 107:19-20

stop, reflect & release

Is there anything that could hinder your healing process?

What is your "why" for healing and becoming whole?

What phase of healing are you in, and what steps can you take to continue progressing?

draw near

Heavenly Father, thank you for bringing me to this place of healing. Search the deep parts of my emotions and heart and bring to light everything I need to surrender to You so I can be made whole and healed. Help me move at Your speed and not mine. Do a complete work in me.

In Jesus' Name, Amen.

LEAN INTO
HEALING

DO YOU HEAR THAT?

That sound....Can you hear it? The sound of your own breath. Even the sound of your heartbeat. There it is again - can you hear it? The silence. It can be deafening.

Seasons of silence can be scary. They can happen gradually or suddenly, and you may wonder: Where did everyone go?! Amid the hustle and bustle, you may sit up to take a breath and suddenly realize the scenery and the people have changed. The sounds that had become familiar and even comforting have been replaced with nothing. This realization alone is enough to send you into a frenzy.

One thing we want to make clear is that we will not believe the enemy's lie that seasons of silence equate to loneliness. We are never and will never be alone! Even in the midst of a season of isolation, insolation, or silence, God is with us! He will never leave us, nor will He ever forsake us. Although seasons of silence can be challenging, they can also have great purpose. Let's chat about the benefits of the silence that seems pointless.

silence at home

Before selling my home, I would eagerly anticipate my family coming to visit because it would fill the empty rooms of my house. My house felt too big, and coming home to an empty house with only me and my young child felt odd. There was no one to share the challenges of the day with or rejoice in the new milestones my son met. I initially kept the TV on in one or two rooms just to have noise in the house. Silence was a space where my thoughts drowned out all other voices. My fears of the future rose like a choker threatening to end any hope or plan for my future.

I'm not sure when the moment of realization came, but I do remember the release that came with this thought: I had lived in so much drama, trauma, and tension in the last nine months to a year that I didn't realize the silence I was avoiding was actually the peace I had been living void of. I ask the same of you: Is it silence or peace? Perhaps it could be both! Silence signals an end to the commotion that was and the entrance of peace ushering us into a new season.

Consider these silent spaces, especially if you have a rotating custody schedule. Think of these silent spaces as an opportunity to rid yourself of built-up stress. Allow the silence to be a blanket of comfort in which you can find rest and peace before the next phase or season of life arrives. Maximize this time to redefine what peace and silence in your home will represent and how it will look.

silence of support

You may find this to be a shocking detail, but I was extremely surprised by the lack of support there was, especially in the faith community, to support those going through divorce. Divorce is still a taboo topic within the faith community; however, I believe it's time to start some conversation and dialogue with divorce rates in the community being so high.

As much as we desire vows to be eternal, whether adversarial forces or poor character and individual decisions, there should be more space for the reality of what people face. There were a faithful few, and I do mean FEW, who regularly checked in with me after finding out I was experiencing divorce. Out of all of the services and years I willingly served with people who felt like family, many bowed out with little encouragement or prayers to offer.

The search may be tedious, but I recommend you look for churches that offer a divorce care programs. This support was a true godsend for me, and I don't even know how I found it on Facebook. This program offered a biblical approach to discussing various topics and situations that arise during the divorce process. It also provided me with community, allowing me to see the faces and hear the voices of those walking through the same season in varying degrees. Although your support may be minimal in this season, be intentional about seeking communities that can support you healthily and biblically.

solitude

Silence can become a place of solitude and a space of torment. Christ is a beautiful example of how time away from people, even the disciples, had purpose. Before testing, Jesus went into a place of solitude for forty days. When he needed to pray and hear the heart of God, he went away from everyone else to seek wisdom and instruction. When he knew he would be facing opposition, he withdrew.

Listen, if Jesus Christ withdrew to a place of solitude throughout his life, how do we think we can function without these moments in our lives? In the midst of trauma and intense emotional experiences, we can see separation and silence as isolation or rejection. But in a healed space, we can better see how these spaces are God's way of drawing us to Him.

When we respond to the draw of God, our mindset and perspective can be shifted. When we draw near to Him, sadness and disappointment can turn into joy and gratitude for God, keeping us with a stable mind and joy since we are now released from that negative space. Resist the urge to push away from God and hide under the covers during this season. Instead, create space for Him in worship and prayer and build your inner man through study in your quiet time. Make your moment of silence a moment of regeneration.

sure ground

This is what the Sovereign Lord, the Holy One of Israel, says: "Only in returning to me and resting in me will you be saved. In quietness and confidence is your strength. But you would have none of it."

ISAIAH 30:15

But Jesus often withdrew to the wilderness for prayer.

LUKE 5:16

stop, reflect & release

How will you redefine peace in this new season?

How will you be intentional about navigating the silent spaces in your life?

What areas in your life need to be addressed if you are avoiding silence?

draw near

Heavenly Father, silence can be a powerful tool for healing or harm. During my seasons of silence, reveal to me when I need rest and to reflect so that the silence doesn't become overwhelming. Help me always remember that You are with me, and I am never alone. Help me understand the purpose of each silent season so I can release unnecessary feelings, emotions, and relationships to gain what You have for me. Help me not to be afraid of the silence.

In Jesus' Name, Amen.

Be strong & courageous. Do not fear or be in dread of them, for it is the Lord your God who goes with you. He will not leave you or forsake you.

DEUTERONOMY 31:6-8

THE SEARCH FOR BETTER DAYS

In my profession as a therapist, I work with families that have experienced traumatic events that occur primarily from freak accidents. In most cases, their typically developing child is now entirely or at least partially dependent on their parent again for care and daily activities. When they arrive at their care team conference, they have one question: "When will all this get better?"

I would imagine those who have gone through a divorce have the same questions. I know I did. I often asked questions throughout the process: When would my life return to normal? When would I start thriving instead of feeling like I am struggling to survive? When will my emotions regulate, and fight no longer be my initial reaction? When will I stop feeling angry? When will I be okay? When will co-parenting be possible? When will this get better?! Unfortunately, we don't know when this season will end. We know that all seasons must end, but that doesn't give us a timeline for this specific season of suffering. I believe it is partly this way so that we surrender the next steps, and even the breaths of our lives, into our all-knowing God's hands. I also believe that by seeking answers to questions, we continue to pursue Him even in the painful moments. I encourage you to ask questions while also calling the nature of God into our minds, saying to Him, "If you work all things together for good, show me the good in this!"

Only God knows what can and will be revealed in our seeking, but almost as if by perfect design, we continue to find Him in that seeking. He can soothe our fears and calm all doubts. Seek first the kingdom, and all these things will be added.

finding closure

Closure is defined as "bringing something to an end" or "the state of being closed." Much of what we will experience during this divorce process could be described as closure: bringing our marriage to a close, bringing broken vows and broken promises to a close, bringing an end to crossed boundaries and broken hearts, etc.

In observation, it seems many people expect closure to look like an apology for our broken hearts or an acknowledgment of wrongdoing. Some may hope for sincere dialogue over lunch to answer questions and erase the memory of nights spent on a tear-filled pillow. But what happens if you do get that "one thing" you've been seeking from your former spouse?

I found that closure came in the form of reflecting over the period of my marriage to see boundaries that need to be checked, repaired, or established. I found closure by knowing I did all that God instructed me to do to seek reconciliation from my marriage. Closing this chapter of my life was so sad and disappointing, dare I say unwanted, to be honest. But to move forward, heal, and be able to live again, I had to come to the sobering reality that this, my marriage, is really over.

That realization can take honesty, courage, boldness, and, most importantly, time. How much time? I don't know. I knew I was forming areas of closure in my life when this happened: My family had planned to come and visit, just my parents, my sister, my brother-in-law, and three nieces. They were very intentional about coming and made sure I was off work on that date. My sister tiptoed around me for a few hours and then stated, "Well, how are you feeling?" I was so confused, and I said, "Fine! What do you mean?" My sister looked around concerned and stated, "Today would have been your anniversary." Shocked, I picked up my phone to indeed see that it was my 4th anniversary!!

Somewhere, the date that used to hang over my head like a stage curtain ready to drop had become a weightless thought fleeting from memory. Somehow, through the strength of God alone, I was closing that chapter and moving on to what was ahead. The sting wasn't there, and I could only laugh in response to not recognizing that date anymore. Even in receiving no apology, even through struggling to establish a co-parenting relationship, I was gaining closure and looking forward to the possibilities ahead.

moving forward

As you will hear repeatedly throughout this book, everyone's process and timeframe will be different. That isn't an inditement anywhere on the spectrum; it's just encouragement to not compare your process to anyone else's. You may move forward in steps and phases while others move forward all at once. Give yourself grace and seek the wisdom of the Lord to know when each move is right for you.

People often state that the front window in a car is larger than the rearview mirror, with the intent of us only reflecting on the past for a short time so we don't miss all the possibilities coming up ahead. The same could be said of our journey through divorce as well. Take all the time you need to feel, cry, scream, breathe, and talk out this experience. Be fully present to sense and feel all this experience will be, but as things shift, don't continue to throw a pity party in areas where God has given you healing and victory!

When we experience victory in our lives, it is our duty and responsibility to go back and get others! Be healed and healthy, but once you are, go free the captives! This journey is not in vain — there will be others that we will encounter who will need our strength and encouragement to make it through a challenging season in their lives. It is our turn to be the light in the darkness, letting them know what we have found out: It DOES get better! Moving forward is possible!

sure ground

Trust in the Lord with all your heart; do not depend on your own understanding. Seek his will in all you do, and he will show you which path to take.

PROVERBS 3:5-6

No, dear brothers and sisters, I have not achieved it, but I focus on this one thing: Forgetting the past and looking forward to what lies ahead, I press on to reach the end of the race and receive the heavenly prize for which God, through Christ Jesus, is calling us.

PHILIPPIANS 3:13-14

For everything there is a season, a time for every activity under heaven.

ECCLESIASTES 3:1

The Lord directs the steps of the godly. He delights in every detail of their lives. Though they stumble, they will never fall, for the Lord holds them by the hand.

PSALMS 37: 23-24

stop, reflect & release

Do you sense that you will find closure all at once or step by step?

Where do you need closure so you can move forward?

What goals or dreams do you have as you move forward?

draw near

Heavenly Father, there will be so many unanswered questions throughout this process. I don't know what will come or how I will get through each phase, but I know and trust You will be with me every day. Heal me where I need healing. Strengthen me when I need strength. When I can't find the answer, help me seek You. Give me peace that surpasses all understanding, even my own.

In Jesus' Name, Amen.

LESS THAN PICTURE-PERFECT

As odd as it seems, when I started going through the divorce process, I became keenly sensitive, almost hyper-aware of others who were going through this same process. As I saw others go through their process, with an attempt to look forward to brighter days, I saw their outcomes and thought: Okay, this is bad. But it can get better!

This search for hope unintentionally became a form of comparison that 1) isn't wise and 2) gave me a false sense of hope—the exact opposite of what I was seeking in the beginning. I quickly learned that what worked for one couple or family through this process may not be the case for me, as factors in my situation varied greatly.

I remain hopeful that better days will come. However, I must figure out how to navigate the current climate with my former spouse. This situation can look very different for everyone, so I encourage you to assess your situation and find 1-2 areas to focus on improving.

year of firsts

My hope is that you will find a cordial and amicable space to function in sooner rather than later, but I also know that people are complex, and the relationships post-divorce can be even more unique. The best outcome would be that you could spend all of your time with your kids or call that former in-law or stepchild to send them well wishes for the "year of firsts" after divorce. This outcome may be the case for some — if so, God bless you! More than likely, this won't be the case for most.

Moving forward, especially when children are involved, it would be wise to make preparations for how you will celebrate holidays, birthdays, and other important events. It is crucial to consider the reality of what this could look like as soon as possible so that when court dates and mediation begin, you have your negotiable and non-negotiables that you can live with.

It was very helpful to establish a plan for all the firsts. In this way, you are intentional with your time and allow little room for the enemy to come in with negative feelings or emotions. This time is also a wonderful opportunity for your village to be your village. If someone calls to invite you, say "yes" even if you show up for only 15 minutes. The "year of firsts" can be challenging, but I encourage you to breathe and take it one step at a time. You will look back and be thankful to God for seeing you through.

make peace

If your situation is anything like mine, then you've definitely heard the term "high-conflict." If there was a reason to argue, we argued. Even if there wasn't a reason to argue, someone would start an argument. Changes in orders and decision-making would spark a flurry of text. You get the picture. There was no peace in the land! I desired a peaceable process moving forward, especially since a child was involved. Realizing that it takes "two to tango" made me rethink my approach to conversations and interactions. It initially required that I humble myself, resist the desire to defend myself, and trust God to defend me. Secondly, I had to remember that "a gentle answer deflects anger" (Proverbs 15:1). I had to quiet my spirit and sincerely ask, "Lord, how should I respond?"

Strategies like being slow to speak, choosing not to respond, or stepping away before responding should be considered in high-conflict situations. If warranted, additional assistance from law enforcement may be required for safety. Our responsibility as believers is to choose to pursue peace when and where there is no peace. Pursuing peace looks like bringing a level of calm and the presence of God in our situation, even if the other party refuses. We are not responsible for their actions and decisions, but we are responsible for our decisions and responses.

Starving the fire of oxygen is the only way to kill the fire — that's how we make peace and get out of the cycle. It takes time, self-control, and trial and error to see what works best for your situation. But I assure you, it is possible, with or without the other party's cooperation. Your emotional and physical health will improve when you can find and walk in that peace.

picture perfect

Picture-perfect conversations and interactions after divorce may be possible for some — that is a blessing.

But for those with more intense situations, for the time being, we must define what our picture-perfect scenario will be. Although this is a negative experience, what are two identifiable things we can "live with"? They may not be the best, but they may be good, and in this season, good is okay and can lead to the best later on.

Soul-searching and deep-digging are encouraged to find the things that really make you tick and pursue those areas with passion! Whether it be custody of children, shared assets, or even nowadays, division of family pets, find what areas you can live with and in peace, and work toward that goal, knowing each story is unique, and the same could be said of each outcome.

Moving forward takes effort and time, but once you are on the other side, you will be grateful for your strides.

sure ground

A gentle answer deflects anger, but harsh words make tempers flare. The tongue of the wise makes knowledge appealing, but the mouth of a fool belches out foolishness.

PROVERBS 15:1-2

But the Holy Spirit produces this kind of fruit in our lives: love, joy, peace, patience, kindness, goodness, faithfulness, gentleness, and self-control. There is no law against these things!

GALATIANS 5:22-23

Oh, don't worry; we wouldn't dare say that we are as wonderful as these other men who tell you how important they are! But they are only comparing themselves with each other, using themselves as the standard of measurement. How ignorant!

2 CORINTHIANS 10:12

stop, reflect & release

What fruit of the spirit do you need to display during high-conflict discussions?

What could be the most peaceable outcome for your situation?

How will you pursue peace? (EX: stopping arguments, focusing discussion on the main topic and not getting personal, etc.)

draw near

Heavenly Father, as I continue to move forward, make me aware of areas I can change that are within my control. Help me not to focus on the other person's behavior or responses but on improving what I can to pursue peace in this situation.

In Jesus' Name, Amen.

BETTER DAYS ARE COMING!

THE REALITY OF FORGIVENESS

Forgiveness brings us to the sobering reality that we, too, have disappointed or hurt others and God, yet graciously, we have received forgiveness. Forgiveness is a difficult task because it requires that we release our intentions and plans for payback or vengeance and that we trust God with the final outcome. It takes the power and control out of our hands and places it back in God's hands. Reconciliation required two people, but forgiveness only needed one.

To be honest, I didn't want to forgive because I felt I didn't deserve all that I had received from my former spouse, which was true. I also thought he didn't deserve forgiveness, which was not true. In the midst of pain and heartache, it can be difficult to remember that our former spouses, despite the pain they've inflicted, are deserving of forgiveness. Take a deep breath because that can be difficult to accept. They, too, deserve forgiveness. Whether the deeds were done consciously or subconsciously, God still welcomes them with the same arms of grace and forgiveness.

what is forgiveness

Forgiveness is something we can offer our former spouse as a means of releasing the hurt, anger, and disappointment that we have experienced by their hand or during the time we spent with them. It allows us to release bitterness and hostility we may hold in our hearts. And it doesn't necessarily require our former spouse to apologize to us to make the decision to forgive.

Forgiveness is not having a sudden case of amnesia, where we pretend nothing happened and no wrongs have occurred. Forgiveness is not excusing our former spouse from being accountable for their actions. Forgiveness is not saying that your healing journey is over and *what will be, will be*. Forgiveness is not a feeling; it is a decision to be obedient to what God has commanded of us so we, too, may be able to receive forgiveness.

unforgiveness unchecked

Hurt can cause someone to feel angry. Without forgiveness, anger can quickly turn into bitterness and a need for revenge - to make the person who hurt us feel the same level of hurt, if not more hurt than we experienced, to make it "even." When we arrive at this place of bitterness, we have the potential to hurt more people than just the individual who hurt us. We take a chance of:

1. Living outside of the will of God for us as believers.

2. Living a life full of pain and suffering as we

rehearse the offenses in our lives.

3. Limiting ourselves from being whole and healed.

I challenge you to take a moment to perform a heart check. Be honest with yourself about whether you've forgiven your former spouse or if you have hindrances in your heart that block your willingness to forgive. Unforgiveness unchecked is far more dangerous than taking the risk to forgive and moving forward in your healing journey. Release them from your idea of payback and give that responsibility to God since He is the only just judge. God is aware of the hurt we've experienced, and He is the only one who can deal with each person justly and appropriately. Freedom is calling, and forgiveness is knocking at the door — will you release the past to take hold of your future?

sure ground

Instead, be kind to each other, tenderhearted, forgiving one another, just as God through Christ has forgiven you.

EPHESIANS 4:32

Make allowance for each other's faults, and forgive anyone who offends you. Remember, the Lord forgave you, so you must forgive others.

COLOSSIANS 3:13

Never pay back evil with more evil. Do things in such a way that everyone can see you are honorable. Do all that you can to live in peace with everyone.

ROMANS 12:17-18

stop, reflect & release

Take time to individually write down offenses of your former spouse that you forgive.

What does walking in forgiveness look like for you?

What do you need to seek forgiveness for?

draw near

Heavenly Father, thank you for the forgiveness You extend to me. Help me be able to forgive my former spouse. I want to surrender the pain that I've experienced to make room for forgiveness so hatred and bitterness have no place to live. Remind me of how much I have been forgiven so I can, in turn, offer that same forgiveness.

In Jesus' Name, Amen.

IT'S ONLY A TEST

One thing that we are assured of is that in this life we will face difficulty. We live in a fallen world, and none of us are immune to difficult times. Scripture also asks how we, as believers, think we will be able to reign with Christ without suffering with him as well. This suffering doesn't mean a literal crucifixion but more so a daily dying to ourselves to take on the life of Christ. We are faced with trials and tribulations as a training ground to give way for us to die to ourselves and take on the mind of Christ. Each difficulty in our lives comes as an opportunity to learn more about our Heavenly Father.

Trials are opportunities that God allows in order to build and exercise our faith muscles, opportunities for us to truly walk out our faith journey. Tribulations come as tests from the enemy sent to distract, distance, or derail us from our faith journey with God. This trial could look like communication challenges, giving us an opportunity to come together and seek wisdom and strategy from the Lord. However, if an offense is caused by how something was expressed, it can become a tribulation, drawing each person further away, which creates space for more offenses to be planted. With offense created, communication from that point can become strained and distant. Then, what used to be a daily conversation can turn into weeks and months of no communication. As persistent as a drop of water on a stone slowly erodes it over time, the same could be said of what can happen in our lives when we give space to the enemy and don't seek God first amid difficulty.

During seasons like this, we must pause and ask, "Did this come from God or the enemy?" With that insight, we will have wisdom on how to walk through that experience.

pop quiz

I'm sure just about everyone has experienced the stress-induced response felt when our school teachers would say, "Okay! Books closed and pencils down! POP QUIZ!" Lord have mercy for real! Hearts began to race, sweat began to gather, and stomachs began to cramp, hoping, wishing, and praying that the information you most recently studied (if you studied) and were exposed to would be accessible to recall.

In all of our anxiety and panic, I think we forgot to remember that pop quizzes never tested us on new information but only included information we have seen, read, or at least attempted before. The same could be said of life. The enemy's tricks are always to steal, kill, or destroy — his tactics may change, but his overall goal remains a tale as old as time. Once you identify him, the next goal is to determine his motive. Although divorce may be undoubtedly one of the worst quizzes of all time, let's take a breath and recall everything we have studied before this. We have had relationships end poorly, yet God remained faithful. We have had disagreements that severed business deals, yet God remained faithful. We may have lost jobs or health at one point, yet God remained faithful. Despite the *subject*, God has remained faithful. So even in this, we will continue to trust God and rely on the faith muscles we have built through each previous season to help us make it through this one. This is how we grow and mature as believers.

sure ground

Dear friends, don't be surprised at the fiery trials you are going through, as if something strange were happening to you. Instead, be very glad—for these trials make you partners with Christ in his suffering, so that you will have the wonderful joy of seeing his glory when it is revealed to all the world. If you are insulted because you bear the name of Christ, you will be blessed, for the glorious Spirit of God rests upon you.

1 PETER 4:12-14

Rejoice in our confident hope. Be patient in trouble, and keep on praying.

ROMANS 12:12

Yet what we suffer now is nothing compared to the glory he will reveal to us later.

ROMANS 8:18

stop, reflect & release

Do you view this season as a trial, tribulation, or both? Why?

What is being tested in your spiritual life?

How will you remain faithful in your relationship with God during this season?

draw near

Heavenly Father, thank you for always being present during every season. As I face each season, please give me wisdom and discernment regarding the type of situation I am facing and how to work through it. Help me seek You first and not any other substitute. Help this be an opportunity for me to grow as a believer and to know You in a new way.

In Jesus' Name, Amen.

DECODING GRIEF

I really can understand why people compare divorce to death. As much as there should have been a "becoming one," likewise, there is a separation of one back to two. There is the death of the relationship. Although the person is still living, there is still a death to the sacred vows and companionship. Secondly, there is the death of the hopes and dreams placed within that marriage. Hopes and dreams of what should have been in growing older together and sharing so many life experiences. At the time, I couldn't fully recognize that I was mourning a variety of things:

- Using our home as a place for small groups and gatherings.
- Raising my son in one place that he would always know as home.
- Being a part of a community.
- Raising my son with his father, modeling a healthy marriage.

- Taking summer family vacations.
- Building equity in our home.
- Developing our backyard into a gathering and meeting place for families and friends.
- Turning our home into an investment property.
- Celebrating all holidays with my son.
- Building businesses with my husband.

The list could go on and on. These are the small things that may not be visible on the outside, but they have a significant impact on our mental and emotional state.

Our lives as believers consist of a sequence of dying to self and living our lives more in the power of Christ. Dying. Gaining life in Christ. Dead. Living again in Christ. And just when you think you have died your last death, there is another new area that requires surrender. My dying came in the form of laying down my vision for my life and my son's life and surrendering our lives to the sovereignty of God. For reasons unclear to me at this time, the prosperity of my marriage was not what God allowed for my life. Be it from a person's decisions or the divine plan of God, it did not prosper. So, even though we wish this cup would pass from us, ultimately, our cry of surrender should be: let Your will be done in us.

shock & denial

Moving out of my house was one of the biggest reality checks for me during my divorce process. In fact, I had moved into my new apartment with 95% of my belongings, but I continued to sleep at my house for another week. The first full week in my apartment felt so strange. I kept saying to myself, "How did I get here? This isn't where I'm supposed to be!"

For some, we never wanted, planned for, or intended for our marriages to end. Even as the ground became shaky, I honestly never saw that the end result would truly be divorce. Even as the divorce was being finalized, I found myself saying, "I am no longer married," or "We are no longer together." The previous two statements left a bitter taste in my mouth personally but seemed to be received a little softer than "I am/We are divorced." When I spoke about a decision that was made or something I'd done with my son, I noticed I often corrected myself by saying, "We decided... I mean, *I decided*" or "We took... I mean, *I took* him to the petting zoo."

Walking through this stage provides an excellent opportunity to begin journaling so that you can process through the '*how did I get here*' moments. Putting words to describe this unfamiliar place may seem daunting, but it makes space for healing work that takes place when we can face these thoughts and feelings instead of burying them inside.

depression

Depression can feel like quicksand. One moment, you're standing on top, and then the next, you are up to your chest, sinking deeper and deeper each second. It can be overwhelming, all-consuming, and downright debilitating. It sneaks up on you and will attempt to hold you captive. And if the enemy of our souls has his way, depression can cause mental instability and utter hopelessness.

To combat depression takes sheer determination and a day-to-day decision not to lose hope. Seek professional help by way of a counselor and/or medication and allow those in your safe community to know how you are struggling so they can surround and support you. One of the most powerful supports for me was forcing myself out of bed, even to the couch, and turning on the Bible on audio or listening to praise and worship music. This push provided just enough hope for me to continue to believe that God would see me through. I would sit outside or in my car during my lunch breaks and do the same thing.

As I spent time in God's presence, I found my strength renewed, my hope restored, and the spirit of heaviness exchanged for a garment of joy. I came to recognize that my "happiness" can falter, but if I hold onto my joy, it can't be taken away!

acceptance

Moving through the processes of grief may come during or after your divorce. Once you have experienced one stage of the grieving process, it does not mean that you won't see it sometime again or in the same sequence that you saw before. The last stage of grieving is acceptance, but I found it to be better described as contentment.

It takes time to settle in and become content in this different, new life. As the grief lifts, God will begin to shift your life from surviving to thriving. The time frame of this shift can vary for everyone, but the key is to find contentment in the highs and the lows — this is how God matures us so that in all seasons, our sure ground is found in Christ and not in our circumstances.

sure ground

He heals the brokenhearted and bandages their wounds.
PSALMS 147:3

You keep track of all my sorrows. You have collected all my tears in your bottle. You have recorded each one in your book.
PSALMS 56:8

Read entire **PSALMS 55**

stop, reflect & release

How have you processed the end of your marriage?

How can you shift your perspective of your new life?

How can you surrender your present and future plans to God?

draw near

Heavenly Father, I am so thankful You are so near to me while I am brokenhearted. Please heal the hurt and wounds that are so painful and, at times, feel all-consuming. I'm thankful that I can cast all of my cares on You, knowing that You care for me and will sustain me. Help me not to get lost in the pain of my situation, but instead, help me persevere during the good times and especially during the hard times. My hope remains in You.

In Jesus' Name, Amen.

UNTOUCHABLE JOY

GUARD YOUR HEART

Maintaining the posture of a clean heart is crucial as you walk through this season. It may not be easy, but it is necessary. A clean heart will aid you in decision-making, maintaining your peace, and being able to forgive, which we discussed in another chapter.

The heart is one of, if not the most, vital organ in the human body. The heart is where the oxygenation and circulation of blood for the entire body begins. It also ensures that waste product (carbon dioxide) is delivered to the lungs to be expelled so it doesn't contaminate the blood or the body. In the same way that a healthy heart maintains the health of the body, a damaged heart has the potential to infect or affect the whole body. If there is irritation to the valves of the heart, it can't pump adequate supply to the other extremities. If the extremities don't receive blood or have poor circulation of blood, they will fail to function properly and begin to die away. The same could be said of our emotional and spiritual selves if we disregard taking care of the matters of our hearts.

guard your heart during healing

Divorce can create a gaping cavern in companionship, personal security, and finances. We can find ourselves in a social or relationship desert. Don't consider this necessarily as a bad thing. This supposed lack could be God's way of protecting and shielding our hearts while we complete our healing process.

With a fresh scrape, you generally want to wash it to clear out any visible debris. Then, you want to keep it clean and dry so healing can begin. During this "set apart" session, it is a perfect time to look around and consider the habits, relationships, and investments (of your time or finances) to see if they aid in your healing or hinder it. A few things I use as a plumb line are considering if they assist in getting me to the destination God had for me, do they build me up, and do they help me keep my mind in on things like the Scripture in Philippians 4:8-9 speaks of:

> And now, dear brothers and sisters, one final thing. Fix your thoughts on what is true, and honorable, and right, and pure, and lovely, and admirable. Think about things that are excellent and worthy of praise. Keep putting into practice all you learned and received from me — everything you heard from me and saw me doing. Then the God of peace will be with you.

Find safe places to refuel and recharge in ways that rebuild you. Fill the new voids with prayer, worship, journaling, and meditation on God's word so that the enemy will not have a place to create any negative emotions that could delay your healing.

guard your heart from opinions

Everyone has an opinion of what they would do in a hypothetical situation. It isn't until you are face-to-face with that very issue that you can determine if your hypothetical plan would work or need modifications. Likewise, in divorce, no one knows the exact journey you've embarked upon. Even those who have experienced divorce will have some degree of variance in their experiences.

Some may say not to speak to your former in-laws, not knowing that you may have had a strong relationship with them before they introduced you to their child. Others may tell you not to invite the former spouse to your child's event unless they ask, but you know it would mean the world to your child to have both parents there. Thoughts and suggestions can easily sway you to the opinions and preferences of man but away from the will of God.

As this process takes place, I encourage you to place your ear as close as possible to the heart of God. He may give you instructions regarding decision-making for your case that may oppose the opinions of close family and friends. He will give you a strategy for speaking to your former spouse to provoke the best outcome in a mediation situation. Following God's divine instruction can bring about a change in the overall outcome of your proceeding that wouldn't have been possible if you followed the opinion and emotion of man.

guard your heart from offense

This process is complicated; there is no disputing that. It brings up painful conversations, reveals some people's true colors, and creates more tension in an already intense situation. During your process, it is essential to remain factual and not move from a place of offense. Using wisdom and strategy from God will trump any vindictive attempt to settle a case.

If children are involved, it is wise to consider the safest plan and the plan that provides the child(ren) an opportunity to know and form a relationship with their other parent. Of course, if safety is a concern, some adjustments should be made, but if that isn't the case, don't allow your disappointment in the outcome of your marriage to be a roadblock to your child(ren) having the opportunity to have both parents or both family sets being present in their lives.

Carrying around offense does nothing to the person who offended you. The person carrying the offense is the one who is blocking healing and restoration in their lives. We desire for our hearts to remain clean and pure so we stay in right standing with God and our prayers won't be hindered.

Discussing matters of the heart during emotionally heightened seasons can be stressful, exhausting, and anxiety-producing. Yet, piece by piece and day by day, we have to make a conscious effort to do the hard work. This effort also includes identifying any guilt or burden we attempt to carry on our own without surrendering it to the Lord. The enemy would have us believe that we can't make it past the weightiness of this moment and that things will never be right again. That is a lie! Is it hard? Yes. Is it impossible? Absolutely NOT! Every time you feel that weight making you weary, bring it back to the feet of the Lord, where we are PROMISED to find rest!

sure ground

Guard your heart above all else, for it determines the course of your life.

PROVERBS 4:23

Create in me a clean heart, O God. Renew a loyal spirit within me.

PSALMS 51:10

Search me, O God, and know my heart; test me and know my anxious thoughts. Point out anything in me that offends you, and lead me along the path of everlasting life.

PSALMS 139: 23-24

Then Jesus said, "Come to me, all of you who are weary and carry heavy burdens, and I will give you rest. Take my yoke upon you. Let me teach you, because I am humble and gentle at heart, and you will find rest for your souls. For my yoke is easy to bear, and the burden I give you is light."

MATTHEW 11: 28-30

stop, reflect & release

What areas in your life are dying or decaying because of your injured heart?

Where are your safe places to recharge and refuel?

What debris needs to be washed out during this season of life?

draw near

Heavenly Father, thank you for the promise of rest for my weary souls. Please help me turn to You and surrender my burdens and weariness in exchange for Your rest. Help me identify what and/or who needs to be removed from my life in this season. Purify my heart and make me aware of anything that is not like You. Thank you for being a safe place.

In Jesus' Name, Amen.

EXTRA Transitioning out of trauma and survival can be a shock to the system. You have spent a decent amount of time (some more than others) just trying to hold your life together as it was seemingly falling apart. It takes such effort to survive that we can forget what living really feels like.

REFRAME YOUR LIFE

I wish I had a way to see into God's future plans and ensure that all will be easy and well. I wish I could promise that everyone who desires to be married again will find an amazing spouse who will cherish and honor them. I don't make those promises because I can't. As much as I hope that people will be able to find restoration, that may not be the case. However, I can assure you that if we remain in fellowship with God, He will guide each step if we submit to His wisdom.

reframe you future

In a previous chapter, we discussed mourning your dreams for your formerly married life so our past wouldn't hold us back and we could move into our healing. The desire to dream again should emerge as we heal and move from surviving to thriving. There isn't a specific timeframe on when this may happen. For me, it was approximately 18 months from when I was first served.

Granted, I was also raising my son, so my process was unique since I had to show up as a parent and heal in my *off time.*

Reframing isn't ignoring or denying what has happened; it is finding the *light* in the midst of *darkness.* Darkness would say, "You are single and have no purpose now that your marriage has ended." Light would say, "Although you are single, you have an opportunity to reignite your passion for helping others and try new hobbies." God has brought us out of darkness and into the marvelous light. We must let that light shine as we testify of the goodness of God!

reframe your self-image

Reframing my self-image involved realizing that what I perceived about my new status was not necessarily what others perceived about me. For example, when traveling, I felt as though people saw me as the single mom struggling to juggle all the luggage and a toddler when most people probably saw a kid and his mom headed out for an adventure.

To deflect attention from myself, I would also dress in sweats or very basic clothing. I didn't want anyone looking in my direction, partly because I felt broken and unwanted. I didn't want people to see the burdens I was carrying. I'd ask you to consider if any of these patterns sound familiar or if you have created your own barriers because your thoughts about yourself and your reflection don't match.

Seeking community support, therapy, and just doing the hard work of renewing my mind were pivotal points in helping me say, "This is something I have experienced.

But I am not my experience!" Using Scriptures that speak to your image in Christ and formation by God is how we renew our minds, exchanging our thoughts for the mind of Christ.

reframe truth

Specifically for people of faith, when we face something that conflicts with our belief system, there tends to be a questioning of faith, a running from faith, or a clinging on to faith. My hope is that we do not turn away from a loving and faithful God in response to disappointments in a person's faithfulness or demonstration of love. Often, our human experiences tend to shape our expectations of how we view God. If bad things happen to us, then God must be upset with us. Instead, we should consider why God has allowed this and who He is creating space for us to be in that experience. So, let's reframe the truth of who God is:

He is the **CREATOR** and **SUSTAINER** of our lives.
He is our loving **FATHER**.
He is our faithful **DEFENDER**.
He is our place of **SHELTER** and **PROTECTION**.
He is the **RESTORER** and giver of **HOPE**.
He is our **PROVIDER**.
He is our **HEALER** and able to give us **BEAUTY** for ashes.
He is the **LIFTER** of our head.
Not only does He give us peace, but He is our **PEACE**!

I encourage you to do something that may seem like a stretch, considering the season you have experienced—reframe your trust in God again! Trust that His plans for you are good, that He is faithful to His word, and that He will redeem the time and things that were stolen.

sure ground

> "For I know the plans I have for you," says the Lord. "They are plans for good and not for disaster, to give you a future and a hope. In those days when you pray, I will listen. If you look for me wholeheartedly, you will find me."
>
> **JEREMIAH 29:11-13**

> And I am certain that God, who began the good work within you, will continue his work until it is finally finished on the day when Christ Jesus returns.
>
> **PHILIPPIANS 1:6**

> The Lord directs the steps of the godly. He delights in every detail of their lives.
>
> **PSALMS 37:23**

reflect & release

What are your fears of the unknown of this new season?

Identify what is within your control, such as eating healthy, and what must be submitted to the will of God, such as the overall outcome of your health.

Find a theme song that introduces this new season of your life.

draw near

Heavenly Father, thank you for helping me endure this challenging season and always remaining with me. I am surrendering my future thoughts and plans to You. Help me fully trust You again. Help me dream again of what can be and what is possible through You. Guide my steps and give me wisdom. And may the truth of who You are be evident in my life.

In Jesus' Name, Amen.

YOUR REDEEMER
LIVES!

JOB 19:25

ABOUT THE AUTHOR

Mariah Willis Strong is a native of Odessa, TX. She is a graduate of Odessa High School and West Texas A & M University (WTAMU) in Canyon, TX, where she was a student-athlete while earning a bachelor's degree in Communication Disorders. She continued her education at WTAMU, earning a master's degree in Communication Disorder.

Mariah was licensed and ordained as a minister through Higher Ground Always Abounding Assemblies while serving at The Potter's House.

She enjoys working within the community as a Speech Language Pathologist and is currently in her 8th year as a chaplain for the Women's National Basketball Association (WNBA).

Author Mariah Willis Strong has been writing since an early age. Through her published works, she desires to find and give hope in the darkest seasons to herself and others. As a licensed and ordained minister, she seeks to bring biblical truth to the reality of today in a palpable way.

Mariah's life's experiences have allowed her to testify, "God is faithful! From not "fitting in" in her formative educational years, to the challenges that came with being a scholarship student-athlete in college, and, more recently, trusting God to navigate her through challenging life journeys, God has been faithful and has kept her through it all.

The highlight of Mariah's life is being the very proud "Mommie" to her busy and loving two-year-old son. Through him, she sees the hand of God teaching her how to raise and nurture him. He is truly a blessing and a witness to God's faithfulness.

CONNECT WITH THE AUTHOR

facebook	facebook.com/mariahwillis87
instagram	@wherehoperemains
tiktok	@wherehoperemains
youtube	Where Hope Remains
podcast	Where Hope Remains

www.ingramcontent.com/pod-product-compliance
Lightning Source LLC
Chambersburg PA
CBHW041628140626
46547CB00031B/1272